First World War
and Army of Occupation
War Diary
France, Belgium and Germany

23 DIVISION
69 Infantry Brigade
Prince of Wales's Own (West Yorkshire Regiment)
11th Battalion
25 August 1915 - 31 October 1917

WO95/2184/4

The Naval & Military Press Ltd
www.nmarchive.com
Published in association with The National Archives

Published by

The Naval & Military Press Ltd

Unit 10 Ridgewood Industrial Park,

Uckfield, East Sussex,

TN22 5QE England

Tel: +44 (0) 1825 749494

www.naval-military-press.com

www.nmarchive.com

This diary has been reprinted in facsimile from the original. Any imperfections are inevitably reproduced and the quality may fall short of modern type and cartographic standards.

© **Crown Copyright**
Images reproduced by permission of The National Archives, London, England, 2015.

Contents

Document type	Place/Title	Date From	Date To
Heading	WO95/2184/4 11th Btn W. York. 1915 Oct-1917 Oct		
Heading	23rd Division 69th Infy Bde 11th Bn West Yorks Regt Oct 1915 1917 Oct To Italy		
Heading	11th West Yorks 23rd Div Vol 12		
War Diary	Southampton	25/08/1915	25/08/1915
War Diary	Havre	26/08/1915	14/09/1915
War Diary	Erquingham	15/09/1915	25/09/1915
War Diary	Trenches	26/09/1915	30/09/1915
Heading	23rd Division 11th West Yorks Vol 3 Oct 15 Mar 19		
War Diary	Trenches	01/10/1915	03/10/1915
War Diary	Estaires	04/10/1915	11/10/1915
War Diary	Trenches	12/10/1915	25/10/1915
War Diary	Fort Rompu	26/10/1915	31/10/1915
Heading	23rd Division 11th W. Yorks Vol : 4 Nov 15		
War Diary	Trenches	01/11/1915	22/11/1915
War Diary	Armentieres	23/11/1915	25/11/1915
War Diary	Hollobeau	26/11/1915	30/11/1915
Heading	11th West Yorks Vol 5 23rd Div		
War Diary	Hollobeau	01/12/1915	31/12/1915
War Diary	Trenches	01/01/1916	02/01/1916
War Diary	Armentieres	03/01/1916	06/01/1916
War Diary	Trenches	07/01/1916	10/01/1916
War Diary	Armentieres	11/01/1916	14/01/1916
War Diary	Jesus Farm	15/01/1916	27/01/1916
War Diary	Trenches	28/01/1916	31/01/1916
War Diary	Erquinghem	01/02/1916	15/02/1916
War Diary	Vieux Berquin	16/02/1916	22/02/1916
War Diary	Estaires	23/02/1916	26/02/1916
War Diary	Steenbecque	27/02/1916	29/02/1916
War Diary	Haillecourt	01/03/1916	05/03/1916
War Diary	Grande Servins	06/03/1916	06/03/1916
War Diary	Trenches	07/03/1916	10/03/1916
War Diary	Grande Servins	11/03/1916	13/03/1916
War Diary	Callonne Ricquart	14/03/1916	22/03/1916
War Diary	Trenches	23/03/1916	31/03/1916
Miscellaneous	G. N. O. A.G. Office 3rd Echelon Rouen. Vol. 6	02/05/1916	02/05/1916
War Diary	Trenches	01/04/1916	16/04/1916
War Diary	Billets	17/04/1916	27/04/1916
War Diary	Billets Coupigny	28/04/1916	30/04/1916
War Diary	Coupigny	01/05/1916	04/05/1916
War Diary	Divion	05/05/1916	31/05/1916
War Diary	Fosse 10	01/06/1916	08/06/1916
War Diary	Bois De Noulette	09/06/1916	13/06/1916
War Diary	Vedrel	14/06/1916	14/06/1916
War Diary	Calonne-Ricouart	15/06/1916	15/06/1916
War Diary	Enquin-Les Mines	16/06/1916	25/06/1916
War Diary	St. Vast-Au-Chaussee.	26/06/1916	30/06/1916
Heading	69th Inf. Bde. 23rd Div. 11th Battn. The West Yorkshire Regiment. July 1916		
War Diary	Coisy	01/07/1916	01/07/1916

War Diary	Bazieux	02/07/1916	02/07/1916
War Diary	Albert	03/07/1916	03/07/1916
War Diary	Scots Redoubt.	04/07/1916	05/07/1916
War Diary	Becourt Wood	06/07/1916	06/07/1916
War Diary	On The March	07/07/1916	08/07/1916
War Diary	Albert	09/07/1916	09/07/1916
War Diary	Trenches	10/07/1916	10/07/1916
War Diary	Albert	11/07/1916	11/07/1916
War Diary	On The March	12/07/1916	13/07/1916
War Diary	Mollien-Au-Bois	14/07/1916	20/07/1916
War Diary	On The March	21/07/1916	21/07/1916
War Diary	Millen Court	22/07/1916	26/07/1916
War Diary	Trenches	27/07/1916	27/07/1916
War Diary	Contalmaison	28/07/1916	31/07/1916
Heading	69th Brigade. 23rd Division. 1/11th Battalion West Yorkshire Regiment August 1916		
War Diary	Albert	01/08/1916	04/08/1916
War Diary	Contalmaison	05/08/1916	07/08/1916
War Diary	Bresle	08/08/1916	11/08/1916
War Diary	Bellancourt	12/08/1916	13/08/1916
War Diary	On The March	14/08/1916	14/08/1916
War Diary	Mount Kokereele	15/08/1916	17/08/1916
War Diary	Steenwerke	18/08/1916	18/08/1916
War Diary	Romarin	19/08/1916	21/08/1916
War Diary	Creslow	22/08/1916	25/08/1916
War Diary	Lewisham Lodge	26/08/1916	30/08/1916
War Diary	Martin Puich	01/10/1916	04/10/1916
War Diary	Trenches Near Le Sars	05/10/1916	07/10/1916
War Diary	Le Sars	08/10/1916	08/10/1916
War Diary	Round Wood	09/10/1916	09/10/1916
War Diary	Albert	10/10/1916	12/10/1916
War Diary	Longpre	13/10/1916	13/10/1916
War Diary	On The March	14/10/1916	15/10/1916
War Diary	Poperinghe	16/10/1916	22/10/1916
War Diary	Ypres	23/10/1916	28/10/1916
War Diary	Trenches	29/10/1916	01/11/1916
War Diary	Ypres	02/11/1916	02/11/1916
War Diary	Salient	03/11/1916	04/11/1916
War Diary	St. Lawrence Camp	05/11/1916	10/11/1916
War Diary	Zillebeeke Bund	11/11/1916	16/11/1916
War Diary	Trenches	17/11/1916	17/11/1916
War Diary	Front Line	18/11/1916	22/11/1916
War Diary	St. Lawrence Camp	23/11/1916	28/11/1916
War Diary	Ypres	29/11/1916	03/12/1916
War Diary	Trenches	04/12/1916	06/12/1916
War Diary	Ypres	07/12/1916	11/12/1916
War Diary	Trenches	12/12/1916	15/12/1916
War Diary	St. Lawrence Camp	16/12/1916	23/12/1916
War Diary	Ypres	24/12/1916	27/12/1916
War Diary	Trenches	28/12/1916	31/12/1916
War Diary	Ypres	01/12/1916	03/12/1916
War Diary	Trenches	04/12/1916	06/12/1916
War Diary	Ypres	07/12/1916	11/12/1916
War Diary	Trenches	12/12/1916	15/12/1916
War Diary	St. Lawrence Camp	16/12/1916	23/12/1916
War Diary	Ypres	24/12/1916	27/12/1916

War Diary	Trenches	28/12/1916	31/12/1916
War Diary	Ypres	01/01/1917	04/01/1917
War Diary	Trenches	05/01/1917	08/01/1917
War Diary	St Lawrence Camp	09/01/1917	15/01/1917
War Diary	Trenches	16/01/1917	20/01/1917
War Diary	Ypres	21/01/1917	24/01/1917
War Diary	Trenches	25/01/1917	28/01/1917
War Diary	Ypres	29/01/1917	31/01/1917
War Diary	Ypres	01/01/1917	04/01/1917
War Diary	Trenches	05/01/1917	08/01/1917
War Diary	St Lawrence Camp	09/01/1917	15/01/1917
War Diary	Trenches	16/01/1917	20/01/1917
War Diary	Ypres	21/01/1917	24/01/1917
War Diary	Trenches	25/01/1917	28/01/1917
War Diary	Ypres	29/01/1917	31/01/1917
War Diary	In The Field	01/02/1917	28/02/1917
War Diary	Merchergem	01/03/1917	01/03/1917
War Diary	Bayenghem	02/03/1917	19/03/1917
War Diary	Merckeghem	20/03/1917	20/03/1917
War Diary	Herzeele	21/03/1917	21/03/1917
War Diary	'Y' Camp	22/03/1917	31/03/1917
War Diary	'Y' Near Near Poperinghe	01/04/1917	06/04/1917
War Diary	Ottawa Camp Nr Poperinghe	07/04/1917	14/04/1917
War Diary	Hill 60	14/04/1917	14/04/1917
War Diary	Ypres Salient	15/04/1917	22/04/1917
War Diary	'Y' Coy Near Poperinghe	01/04/1917	06/04/1917
War Diary	Ottawa Camp N. Poperinghe	07/04/1917	14/04/1917
War Diary	Hill 60	14/04/1917	14/04/1917
War Diary	Ypres Salient.	15/04/1917	30/04/1917
War Diary		23/04/1917	30/04/1917
War Diary	Steen Voorde	01/05/1917	18/05/1917
War Diary	Zillebeke Bund	19/05/1917	24/05/1917
War Diary	Boeschepe	25/05/1917	31/05/1917
War Diary	Steen Voorde	01/05/1917	17/05/1917
War Diary	Zillebeke Bund	18/05/1917	31/05/1917
Miscellaneous	Headquarters, 69th Infantry Brigade.	06/07/1917	06/07/1917
War Diary	Boschepe	01/06/1917	01/06/1917
War Diary	L.33.d.1.G.	02/06/1917	02/06/1917
War Diary	L. Camp	03/06/1917	03/06/1917
War Diary	Zillebeke Bund	04/06/1917	04/06/1917
War Diary	Hill 60	05/06/1917	12/06/1917
War Diary	Meteren Area	13/06/1917	28/06/1917
War Diary	Ontario Camp	29/06/1917	29/06/1917
War Diary	Battle Wood Sub Sector	30/06/1917	30/06/1917
War Diary	Battle Wood Sub Sector Of Line	01/07/1917	31/08/1917
Heading	War Diary 11th Batt West Yorks Regt. September 1917		
War Diary	Chateau Segard	01/09/1917	01/09/1917
War Diary	Steenvoorde	02/09/1917	02/09/1917
War Diary	Lederzeele	03/09/1917	12/09/1917
War Diary	Steenvoorde	13/09/1917	13/09/1917
War Diary	Ontario Camp	14/09/1917	15/09/1917
War Diary	Micmac Camp	16/09/1917	30/09/1917
Heading	Orders For The Attack Issued By Lieut. Col. M.G.H. Barker. D.S.O. Commanding 11th Bn West Yorkshire Regiment.		

Operation(al) Order(s)	Operation Order No 1 By Major H.H. Hudson M.C. Commanding 11th Bn West Yorkshire Regt.	13/09/1917	13/09/1917
Miscellaneous Map			
Miscellaneous	Message Form.		
Operation(al) Order(s)	Additions To Operation Order No. 1		
Operation(al) Order(s)	Appendix "A" To Operation Order No. 1	17/09/1917	17/09/1917
Heading	Battle Of Menin Road Attack By 23rd Division Preparation For The Attack.		
Miscellaneous	Coy. 11th Bn West Yorkshire Regt.	17/09/1917	17/09/1917
Miscellaneous	To The C.O. 11th Bn West Yorkshire Regt	17/09/1917	17/09/1917
Miscellaneous	D Coy 11th West Yorks Reg.	17/09/1917	17/09/1917
Miscellaneous	A Form. Messages And Signals.		
Miscellaneous	H.Q. Cable.		
Miscellaneous	O.C. 11th W. Yorks R.		
Miscellaneous	O.C. 11th W. Yorks		
Miscellaneous	O.C. 11th W. Yorks.	21/09/1917	21/09/1917
Miscellaneous	A Form. Messages And Signals.		
Miscellaneous	B Coy 11th Bn West Yorks Regt.	24/09/1917	24/09/1917
Miscellaneous	To Adjutant 11th West Yorks Regt.	25/09/1917	25/09/1917
Miscellaneous	A Company Casualty Report 25/9/17	25/09/1917	25/09/1917
Miscellaneous	C. Coy 11th West Yorks Regt	25/09/1917	25/09/1917
Miscellaneous	11th West Yk. R.	30/09/1917	30/09/1917
Heading	The Attack In Progress		
Miscellaneous	C Form. Messages And Signals.		
Miscellaneous	A Form. Messages And Signals.		
Miscellaneous	C Form. Messages And Signals.		
Miscellaneous	A Form. Messages And Signals.		
Miscellaneous	C Form. Messages And Signals.	20/09/1917	20/09/1917
Miscellaneous	C Form. Messages And Signals.		
Miscellaneous	Headquarters		
Miscellaneous	Cable.		
Miscellaneous	C Form. Messages And Signals.		
Miscellaneous	Message Pad		
Miscellaneous			
Miscellaneous	A Form. Messages And Signals.		
Miscellaneous	C Form Messages And Signals		
Miscellaneous	C Form. Messages And Signals.		
Miscellaneous	To Sand		
Miscellaneous			
Miscellaneous	C Form. Messages And Signals.		
Heading	Casualties		
Miscellaneous	D. Company 11th (S) Batt. West. Yorkshire. Regt. Battle Casualties.		
Miscellaneous	Operation Instructions By Lieut-Colonel F.W. Lethbridge Commanding 10th. Battalion Duke Of Wellington S Regiment.		
Miscellaneous			
Miscellaneous		18/09/1917	18/09/1917
War Diary	Inverness Copse Sector	01/10/1917	01/10/1917
War Diary	Ridge Wood	02/10/1917	02/10/1917
War Diary	Berthen Area	03/10/1917	08/10/1917
War Diary	Reninghelst.	09/10/1917	09/10/1917
War Diary	Dickebusch	10/10/1917	10/10/1917
War Diary	Clapham Junction	11/10/1917	11/10/1917
War Diary	Front Line	12/10/1917	15/10/1917

War Diary	Zillebeke Bund	16/10/1917	16/10/1917
War Diary	English Wood	17/10/1917	19/10/1917
War Diary	Zillebeke Bund	19/10/1917	19/10/1917
War Diary	Front Line	20/10/1917	22/10/1917
War Diary	Zillebeke Bund	22/10/1917	22/10/1917
War Diary	Wizernes	23/10/1917	23/10/1917
War Diary	Moringhem	24/10/1917	31/10/1917

WO 95 2184/4

11th Bn W.York.

1915 OCT — 1917 OCT

23RD DIVISION
69TH INFY BDE

11TH BN WEST YORKS REGT

OCT 1915 ~~MAR 1918~~

1917 OCT

TO ITALY

69/23

11ᵗᵉ Werk
Jahr
1883

Vol. 2

Army Form C. 2118

WAR DIARY
or
INTELLIGENCE SUMMARY
(Erase heading not required.)

Place	Date	Hour	Summary of Events and Information	Remarks and references to Appendices
SOUTHAMPTON	Aug 25th	5.30pm	Commenced entraining.	
	" 26th	6.20pm	Left SOUTHAMPTON on S.S. Mona's Queen.	
HAVRE		6.45am	Disembarked & proceeded to Rest Camp No. 2.	
	" 27.	12.30pm	Marched from Rest Camp No. 2. to No 1 point Gare du Merchandise.	
		5.pm	Entrained	
		5.30pm	Left LE HAVRE.	
	28th	9am.	Arrived & detrained at WATTEN & marched to BAYENGHAM.	
		1pm	Arrived in billets at BAYENGHAM.	
	29th		In billets at BAYENGHAM. Church Parade in morning.	
	30		" " Route march in morning.	
	31st		" " " "	
	Sept 1st		" " " "	
	2nd		Divisional Tactical Exercise.	
	3rd		In billets at BAYENGHAM	
	4th		" " "	
	5th		Sunday in billets at BAYENGHAM. Received orders to move.	
	6th	6.15am	Marched from BAYENGHAM. Billets for night at SERCUSE.	
	7th	7.45am	SERCUSE. Arrive and billet at DOULIEU.	
	8th		Rest in billets at DOULIEU Inspection of Bn by General Pulteney	
	9th	9.20am	Left DOULIEU, arrive & bivouac on RUE DELPIERRE. S. of ERQUINGHAM at 5pm	
	10th	9 am.	Bn H.Q. 9 O.i.C Coys go up to trenches held by 2nd A.+ S.H. at 2.pm.	
		1.30.pm.	A+B Coys move into trenches for individual instruction under 2nd A.Y.S.H	
		7.10pm	Bn H.Q. & A+B Coys move into trenches for individual instruction under 2nd Gloucesters. Other Officers & N.C.O's Lecture under 2nd Gloucesters.	

Army Form C. 2118

Instructions regarding War Diaries and Intelligence Summaries are contained in F. S. Regs., Part II and the Staff Manual respectively. Title Pages will be prepared in manuscript.

WAR DIARY
or
INTELLIGENCE SUMMARY
(Erase heading not required.)

Place	Date	Hour	Summary of Events and Information	Remarks and references to Appendices
	Sept. 10th	9.30pm	Bursts of rapid fire from enemy trenches otherwise quiet night.	Men slept well.
	11th		A & B quiet day in trenches. C & D bivouacs under 2nd Gloucesters	
		7.10pm	A & B. leave trenches.	
		8pm	C & D. go in trenches.	
		10.30am	A & B Coys marched from bivouac arriving in billets at DOULIEU at 3.30pm	
	12th		Received Draft. 1 Sergt. 1 A/Cpl. 96 Ptes.	
		7.10pm	C & D marched from trenches arriving DOULIEU 2.30am	
	13th		Rest in billets	
	14th		In billets at DOULIEU. received orders to move.	
ERQUINGHAM	13th		Moved to billets in RUE DELETTRE - ERQUINGHAM	
	16th		(Remained in billets)	
	17th		do	Provided working parties
	18th		do	800–900 men every
	19th		do	night in trenches
	20th		do	continued
	21st		Bombardment of enemy's position commenced	do. 1st Casualty. 1 Pte killed
	22		do	do. shrapnel on entry
	23		Rainy do	do. July
	24		Rainy do	by 6th Division
	25	4.30am	Final bombardment & attack on enemy's position Stood to Arms 4.15am.	
			Weather fine & cold wind S.W. then misty. Remained in billets	
			Stood to Arms. Quiet day. Remained in billets until 6.45pm. when consequent	
			on orders from 69 Bde. the Battalion moved to trenches in relief of	
TRENCHES	26	4.30am	10th West Riding Regt. Relief much hampered by mud in the trenches &	
			bad roads to communication trench. Occupied trenches 52, 53, 54, Y.5, Y.5.54	
			Relief complete 10.45pm. Quiet night. Some sniping. Patrols & listening patrols out.	
			No enemy seen.	

1875 Wt. W593/826 1,000,000 4/15 J.B.C. & A. A.D.S.S./Forms/C. 2118.

Army Form C. 2118

WAR DIARY
or
INTELLIGENCE SUMMARY

(Erase heading not required.)

Instructions regarding War Diaries and Intelligence Summaries are contained in F. S. Regs., Part II. and the Staff Manual respectively. Title Pages will be prepared in manuscript.

Place	Date	Hour	Summary of Events and Information	Remarks and references to Appendices
TRENCHES	27th	4.0 a.m	Stood to Arms. During the day some artillery fire from enemy. H.V. shells chiefly, no damage. Quiet day – sniping but nothing else.	
	28th	4.0 a.m	Stood to Arms. Day very quiet – some sniping, artillery fire very small. weather fair – some rain.	
	29th	4.0 a.m	Stood to Arms. Day very quiet, a small amount artillery fire, very wet.	
	30th	4.15 am	Stood to Arms. Quiet day though a good deal of sniping went on throughout the day and night.	

J Blackwell Capt.
Adjutant,
11th (Service) Bn. West Yorkshire Regt.

23rd Kraun

12/
7595

11 To West Yollo
Vol 3

Oct 15 / Mar 19

Q

Army Form C. 2118.

WAR DIARY
or
INTELLIGENCE SUMMARY.
(Erase heading not required.)

Instructions regarding War Diaries and Intelligence Summaries are contained in F.S. Regs., Part II and the Staff Manual respectively. Title pages will be prepared in manuscript.

Place	Date	Hour	Summary of Events and Information	Remarks and references to Appendices
TRENCHES	Oct. 1st		Battalion in the trenches - nothing of importance occurred - the usual work on repairs of parapets during the day and at night. The trenches and defences were worked at. Patrols moved out at night but no contact with the enemy. Weather wet and chilly. Clear & frosty at night.	
	2nd		Battalion in trenches a quiet day - Relief of Battalion took place in the evening by the 10th Northumberland Fusiliers - the relief commenced at 7 p.m. & was concluded at 10.45 p.m. Great delay caused by the bad state of the communicating trenches, thick slippery mud made movement very slow. Fine clear day, frost at night. Marched to Billets for the night in the vicinity of Square B.26.d.	
	3rd		Transferred to ESTAIRES for attachment to 20th Division temporarily - Billets	
ESTAIRES	4th		Billets - Alarm at 4.30 a.m. for instant movement - order cancelled at 6 a.m.	

Army Form C. 2118.

WAR DIARY
or
INTELLIGENCE SUMMARY.
(Erase heading not required.)

Instructions regarding War Diaries and Intelligence Summaries are contained in F. S. Regs., Part II. and the Staff Manual respectively. Title pages will be prepared in manuscript.

Place	Date	Hour	Summary of Events and Information	Remarks and references to Appendices
ESTAIRES.	Oct. 5th		Billets	
	6th		ditto	
	7th		ditto	
	8th		ditto	
	9th		ditto	
	10th		ditto	
	11th		Left ESTAIRES at 9.30 a.m. en route to trenches 63.64.65.66. Halted at JESUS FARM. B.36.d.3. at 11 a.m. & proceeded thence to trenches at 5 p.m. Relieved 2nd K.O.Y.L.I. in trenches, relief commenced 7.30 p.m. & was completed at 10 p.m. hostile situation in trenches no movement of the enemy.	
TRENCHES.	12th		STAND TO. 4.45 a.m. till 6 a.m. Quiet day no activity on part of enemy. Enemy working party dispersed by machine gun fire at 9.30 p.m. rest of night passed quietly.	
	13th		Day quiet until 5.30 p.m. when enemy shelled this trenches, fitted little damage done, shells fell 5 chiefly in front & in rear of trenches night normal nothing to report.	

2353 Wt. W2544/1454 700,000 5/15 D. D. & L. A.D.S.S./Forms/C. 2118.

Army Form C. 2118.

WAR DIARY
or
INTELLIGENCE SUMMARY.
(Erase heading not required.)

Instructions regarding War Diaries and Intelligence Summaries are contained in F. S. Regs., Part II. and the Staff Manual respectively. Title pages will be prepared in manuscript.

Place	Date	Hour	Summary of Events and Information	Remarks and references to Appendices
TRENCHES.	Oct 14th		Situation normal – enemy very quiet. Weather fair, foggy during night & early morning. During the night an enemy working party was dispersed by machine gun fire opposite trenches I.16.2 & I.16.	
	15th		Enemy very quiet during the day. At about 7.30 pm a few enemy shells fell in our lines doing no material damage. During the night our machine guns fired at enemy working party opposite trench I.15.1. also at enemy searchlights. Weather fair, foggy during night & early morning.	
	16th		Day very quiet. at 4.30 p.m the enemy shelled our front trenches, about 20 high explosive & shrapnel shells falling in front & in rear of our trenches, very little damage done. At 7 p.m the Battalion was relieved by the 10th S.Bn WEST RIDING REGT. & took their place in the trenches Bois GRENIER line trenches.	Bois GRENIER
	17th		Bn. GRENIER. a few enemy shells burst behind our trenches at about 3 p.m.	

WAR DIARY
or
INTELLIGENCE SUMMARY.
(Erase heading not required.)

Army Form C. 2118.

Place	Date	Hour	Summary of Events and Information	Remarks and references to Appendices
TRENCHES	Oct 18th		BOIS GRENIER. Our front line nothing to report. Work on dug outs & trenches.	
	19th		Our front line. About 2.30 pm 6 enemy shells burst behind our line & one in trench doing a slight amount of damage.	
	20th		BOIS GRENIER. On our front line. Advance patrols went up to take over trenches in German front line opposite Rue du Bois salient I.22.–I.21.1.–I.21.2.–I.21.3. from 9th K.S.B. & Yorkshire Regt. Relieved 9th YORKSHIRE REGt. in trenches at 7.30 p.m. (front line) & right flank of very quietly. Double sentries posted went hard on German front line salient. Very quiet until 4.30 p.m. when enemy bombarded our salient with trench mortars. 30 bombs falling behind our fire trenches. Our artillery replied with excellent effect. Enemy trying to enemy, whose artillery only fired a few (about 20 rounds) into our trenches doing no damage. The night passed quietly.	
	21st		C & D Coys 11th West Yorkshire Regt. moved into billets in the Rue Marle to be attached to the 2nd EAST LANCASHIRE REGt. their C & D Coys replacing them in the trenches.	

Army Form C. 2118.

WAR DIARY
or
INTELLIGENCE SUMMARY.
(Erase heading not required.)

Place	Date	Hour	Summary of Events and Information	Remarks and references to Appendices
TRENCHES	Oct 22nd		Day quiet – Our artillery registered during the afternoon. During the night the enemy appeared nervous sending up frequent bursts of machine gun & rapid rifle fire	
	23rd		Day very quiet no shelling very little rifle or machine gun fire – During the night patrols went out – no contact with the enemy.	
	24th		Quiet day – During the night ground between lines & German wire were examined by patrols, one of our men being wounded by a shot from a German patrol who were fired at & disappeared.	
	25th		Day quiet – raining hard. Advance parties of the 2nd NORTHAMPTONSHIRE REGT came to take over trenches – 8 pm Battalion relieved in the trenches by 2nd NORTHANTS – A & B Coys 11th WEST YORKSHIRE REGT marched to billets at FORT ROMPU – C & D Coys 2nd EAST LANCS rejoined their unit relieving C & D Coys 11th WEST YORKSHIRE REGT who rejoined Battalion in billets.	

Army Form C. 2118.

WAR DIARY
or
INTELLIGENCE SUMMARY.
(Erase heading not required.)

Place	Date	Hour	Summary of Events and Information	Remarks and references to Appendices
FORT ROMPU	Oct			
	26th		In billets	
	27th		"	
	28th		"	
	29th		" marched to bivouac in afternoon & relieved the 2nd NORTHAMPTONSHIRE REGT in trenches I.26.2-I.21.1-I.21.7-I.21.3. Night exceptionally quiet.	
	30th		Day passed quietly - our artillery registered at various times - our patrols moved out as far as the German wire but met no enemy - look on wire. Weather fine	
	31st		Day quiet - during the night enemy more active than usual frequently sweeping our parapet with search-light & machine gun fire our machine guns replied with unknown effect. Weather wet.	

Signed G. Leh
Lieut 11th West Yorkshire Regt
Comdg 11th [?]
3-11-15

23rd Kirkcudbr 11th W. Yorks |C|
vol: 4   7656

Nov. 15.

Army Form C. 2118.

WAR DIARY
or
INTELLIGENCE SUMMARY.
(Erase heading not required.)

Instructions regarding War Diaries and Intelligence Summaries are contained in F. S. Regs., Part II. and the Staff Manual respectively. Title pages will be prepared in manuscript.

Place	Date	Hour	Summary of Events and Information	Remarks and references to Appendices
TRENCHES.	Nov. 1st		Enemy very quiet all day & during the night — Heavy rain the night was spent in repairing parapets & parados which had fallen in owing to the wet.	
	2nd.		Enemy very quiet — very wet weather — relieved by the 9th S. Bn Yorkshire Regt in the evening & took up position in BOIS GRENIER LINE S. Trenches.	
	3rd		In BOIS GRENIER LINE Support trenches.	
	4th		do.	
	5th		do.	
	6th		do.	
	7th		ARMENTIERES in evening.	
	8th		Billets	
	9th		do	
	10th		do	
	11th		do	
			do. proceeded to billets in Rue Marle	
			the Trenches (I.20.2, I.21.1, I.21.2, I.21.3) Relieved 9th S. Bn Yorkshire Regt in the evening.	

Army Form C. 2118.

WAR DIARY
or
INTELLIGENCE SUMMARY.
(Erase heading not required.)

Instructions regarding War Diaries and Intelligence Summaries are contained in F.S. Regs., Part II. and the Staff Manual respectively. Title pages will be prepared in manuscript.

Place	Date	Hour	Summary of Events and Information	Remarks and references to Appendices
TRENCHES.	Nov. 12th		Day & night very quiet with the exception of burst of enemy machine gun & rapid rifle fire which was replied to — Enemy working party dispersed by our machine guns at about 11.30 p.m. Weather very wet — much time spent in repairing damage done to trenches by weather.	
	13th		Day very quiet — during the night occasional burst of enemy machine gun & rifle fire which were replied to. Enemy very quiet — during the night occasional bursts of rapid fire were opened on the enemy's parapet our machine gunners harassing when the enemy replied.	
	14th		Day very quiet — relieved by 9th S.B. Yorkshire Regt. in the Trenches in evening & took up position in BOIS GRENIER LINE	
	15th		Support Trenches	
	16th		Support Trenches	
	17th		do	
	18th		do relieved 9th Y.S.B. Yorkshire Regt. in evening.	

I.20.2. I.21.1, I.21.2, I.21.3. in evening.

Army Form C. 2118.

WAR DIARY
OR
INTELLIGENCE SUMMARY.
(Erase heading not required.)

Instructions regarding War Diaries and Intelligence Summaries are contained in F. S. Regs., Part II. and the Staff Manual respectively. Title pages will be prepared in manuscript.

Place	Date	Hour	Summary of Events and Information	Remarks and references to Appendices
TRENCHES.	19th		Quiet day – a good deal of rifle & machine gun fire during the night due to the bright moon, weather clear & frosty.	
	20th		Very quiet indeed nothing to report.	
	21st		Quiet day – during the night enemy machine guns very active, rifle fire normal.	
	22nd		Day quiet – in the afternoon turned I.21.3 and handed over to the 10th S. B. West Riding Regt & Trenches I.20.1 & I.26.5 were taken over from the 1st Bn Notts & Derby Regt. Relieved by 9th S. B. Yorkshire Regt in Trenches I.26.5, I.20.1. I.20.2, I.21.1. & I.21.2 in evening & proceeded to Billets in Rue Marle ARMENTIERES	
ARMENT -IERES	23rd		Billets	
	24th		do.	
	25th		do.	
HOLLOBEAU	26th		marched to Billets at HOLLOBEAU in evening.	
	27th		Billets do.	

Army Form C. 2118.

WAR DIARY
or
INTELLIGENCE SUMMARY.
(Erase heading not required.)

Place	Date	Hour	Summary of Events and Information	Remarks and references to Appendices
HOLLDREAU	28th		Billets	
	29th		do.	
	30th		do.	

L C Bedwell Lt Colonel,
Commanding 11th (Service) Bn. West Yorkshire Regt.

11th West
Jenks
Vol 45
23 D 3

Army Form C. 2118.

WAR DIARY
or
INTELLIGENCE SUMMARY.
(Erase heading not required.)

Place	Date	Hour	Summary of Events and Information	Remarks and references to Appendices
HOLLEBEKE	1.12.15		In Billets	
	2.12.15		do	
	3.12.15		do	
	4.12.15		do	
	5.12.15		do	
	6.12.15		Relieved WORCESTER REGT in Trenches I.31.1. I.31.2. I.31.3. I.31.4. & I.31.5 in front of BOIS GRENIER. 10th WEST RIDING REGIMENT on our left and the 20th DIVISION on our right. Enemy very quiet - Trenches very wet.	
	7.12.15		During the day enemy were very quiet. Our artillery damaged the enemy parapet opposite I.31.1. Enemy observers over the parapet frequently. They were dressed in a drab uniform and wore spiked helmets.	
	8.12.15		An enemy searchlight was used opposite Trench I.31.2. The water in the trenches has been considerably reduced by the aid of the pumps.	

Army Form C. 2118.

WAR DIARY
or
INTELLIGENCE SUMMARY.
(Erase heading not required.)

Instructions regarding War Diaries and Intelligence Summaries are contained in F.S. Regs., Part II. and the Staff Manual respectively. Title pages will be prepared in manuscript.

Place	Date	Hour	Summary of Events and Information	Remarks and references to Appendices
	1915			
	9.12.15	12.40 p.m	Enemy fired about 30 H.E. Shells which burst just E of White City - doing no material damage. Our artillery retaliated and silenced the enemy. Relieved by 9th (S) Bn Yorkshire Regiment, on completion of which we moved back into billets in RUE DELETTREE	
	10.12.15		In Billets	
	11.12.15		" "	
	12.12.15		" "	
	13.12.15		" "	
	14/12/15		Relieved 9th (S) Bn Yorkshire Regt in Trenches I.31.1. to I.31.5. Relief completed at 5.44 p.m. Enemy fired an unusual number of flares at regular intervals. Enemy very quiet. No disturbance occurred as a result of the operations carried out by 20th Division at 2 a.m.	
	15.12.15		Very quiet.	
	16.12.15			
	17.12.15	6	A party of Germans about 40 strong was reported by a patrol to have climbed our parapet and peered up into the parados. Garrison stood to arms till 10.20 p.m. but nothing happened. No flares were sent up by the enemy during the time.	
	18.12.15		Relieved by 9th (S/B) Yorkshire Regt. Bn moved into Billets in Rue DELETTREE	

Army Form C. 2118.

WAR DIARY
or
INTELLIGENCE SUMMARY.
(Erase heading not required.)

Place	Date	Hour	Summary of Events and Information	Remarks and references to Appendices
	19/10/15		In Billets	
	20/10/15		"	
	21/10/15		"	
	22/10/15		Btn moved into divisional reserve after relief by 68th Brigade. "B" moved into Billets at FORT ROMPU	
	23/10/15		In Billets	
	24/10/15		"	
	25/10/15		"	
	26/10/15		"	
	27/10/15		"	
	28/10/15		"	
	29/10/15		Relieved 2nd Northants Regiment in Trenches I 26.5. I 20.1. I 20.2. I 20.1. I 20.2.2 Two Companies and four machine guns were holding the front line, two Companies and two machine guns were in reserve in BOIS GRENIER line. The two reserve machine guns were found by C Battalion but manned by our Battalion. Relief completed at 7.6 pm	

Army Form C. 2118

WAR DIARY
or
INTELLIGENCE SUMMARY
(Erase heading not required.)

Place	Date	Hour	Summary of Events and Information	Remarks and references to Appendices
	1915 30/12/15		Enemy used his Small Searchlight during the night. They appeared to be behind the front line opposite Trench I 20.d. the position of the lights was changed constantly.	
	31/12/15		The day passed quietly. the usual amount of sniping going on.	

J.G. Bedwell
Adjutant
10th (Service) Bn. West Yorkshire Regt.

Vol 6 Army Form C. 2118
- 1/4th Yorks

WAR DIARY
or
INTELLIGENCE SUMMARY
(Erase heading not required.)

Place	Date	Hour	Summary of Events and Information	Remarks and references to Appendices
	January 1916.			
TRENCHES	1.1.16.		This batt holding TRENCHES I.26.5 – I.20.1. – I.20.2. – I.21.1. & I.21.2. West Riding Regt on our left. Day & night very quiet nothing to report. Enemy quiet.	
	2.1.16		Day quiet with the exception of 30 minutes heavy shelling at 12 noon the majority of the shells fell around Bn HQ at BURNT FARM & DEAD COW FARM. Relieved by the 9th Yorkshire Regt in trenches in the evening & proceeded to billets in RUE MARLE ARMENTIÈRES	
ARMENT-IERES	3.1.16 4.1.16 5.1.16 6.1.16		do do do	
			Relieved 9th Yorkshire Regt in the trenches in the night very quiet nothing to report. Enemy quiet.	
TRENCHES	7.1.16		Quiet day, very little shelling, no machine gun fire enemy snipers have been active than usual	
	8.1.16		Quiet day, the enemy shelled BURNT FARM & DEAD COW FARM for ½ an hour at mid day, with about 30 high velocity shells doing no damage. Nothing else to report.	
	9.1.16.		Quiet day enemy snipers less active than usual no shelling, during the night our machine gun fired on three enemy working parties, causing them to cease work.	

1875 Wt. W 593/326 1,000,000 4/15 J.B.C. & A. A.D.S.S./Forms/C. 2118.

WAR DIARY
or
INTELLIGENCE SUMMARY
(Erase heading not required.)

Army Form C. 2118

Instructions regarding War Diaries and Intelligence Summaries are contained in F. S. Regs, Part II. and the Staff Manual respectively. Title Pages will be prepared in manuscript.

Place	Date	Hour	Summary of Events and Information	Remarks and references to Appendices
TRENCHES	10.1.16		Quiet day very little rifle fire – no shelling. Relieved by 8th YORKSHIRE REGT in the trenches in the evening & proceeded to billets in the RUE MARLE. ARMENTIERES	
ARMENTI- ERES	11.1.16		Billets	
	12.1.16		ditto	
	13.1.16		ditto	
	14.1.16		Marched to billets in Divisional Reserve at JESUS FARM on the NIEPPE – CROIX DU BAC Road. in the evening.	
JESUS FARM	15.1.16		Billets	
	16.1.16		"	
	17.1.16		"	
	18.1.16		"	
	19.1.16		"	
	20.1.16		"	
	21.1.16		"	
	22.1.16		"	
	23.1.16		marched to billets in Brigade Reserve in RUE DE LETTRE.G in the evening.	
	24.1.16		billets	
	25.1.16		"	
	26.1.16		"	
	27.1.16		Relieved 9th YORKSHIRE REGT in the Trenches I.31.1 to I.31.5 in front of BOIS GRENIER. 2 Coys of the 16th ROYAL SCOTTS accompanied this unit to the trenches for instructions.	

WAR DIARY
or
INTELLIGENCE SUMMARY

Army Form C. 2118

Place	Date	Hour	Summary of Events and Information	Remarks and references to Appendices
TRENCHES	28.1.16		At 6.15 a.m the Bde on our right made a demonstration against the enemy, our right Company assisted by bursts of rapid fire. The enemy retaliated slightly with Whiz Bangs on our right doing no damage. Remainder of the day quiet, with the exception of intermittent shelling of our communication & support trenches during the afternoon, no material damage was done on both sides	
	29.1.16		Day quiet - no shelling - snipers active on both sides night normal	
	30.1.16		Day very misty - a considerable amount of random rifle fire during the afternoon. The enemy fired a few rifle grenades into our left Company & shots from our right Company from 10. p.m to 1.30 a.m [31.1.16] Lts B.H. Story & Amos in conjunction with a minor operation to be carried out by the 1st W. RIDING REGT on our left.	
	31.1.16		Day quiet nothing to report. Relieved by the 9th YORKSHIRE REGT. In evening the 2 Coys of the 16th ROYAL SCOTTS attached reserve of their unit on completion. This unit proceeded to reserve billets in RUE DE LETTRÉE	

J.P. Rockwill Capt
& Adjutant.
11th (Service) Bn. West Yorkshire Regt.

Army Form C. 2118

No 7 11th W Yorks

WAR DIARY
or
INTELLIGENCE SUMMARY

(Erase heading not required.)

Place	Date	Hour	Summary of Events and Information	Remarks and references to Appendices
ERQUINGHEM	1.2.16		*February 1916.* In reserve billets in RUE DE LETTREE	
	2.2.16		ditto	
	3.2.16		ditto	
	4.2.16		Marched to trenches I31.1 to I31.5 in front of BOIS GRENIER in evening + relieved 9th YORKSHIRE REGT in the trenches the night passed quietly	
	5.2.16		The enemy snipers more active than usual along our front, a considerable amount of fire from fixed rifles during the night often into nothing to report.	
	6.2.16		Day very quiet, our snipers were active, enemy snipers quieter no shelling — night normal.	
	7.2.16		Enemy very quiet all day + night during the night our machine guns defenced enemy working parties opposite the BRIDOUX SALIENT.	
	8.2.16		At 6 a.m. our centre Coy (trench) bombs into the enemy saps head on the BRIDOUX Road ones were feared. Remainder of the day very quiet. Relieved by the 13th DURHAM LIGHT INFANTRY. In the evening proceeded to billets in RUE DORMOIRE near FORT ROMPU in Divisional Reserve.	
	9.2.16		Billets	
	10.2.16		" "	
	11.2.16		" "	
	12.2.16		" "	

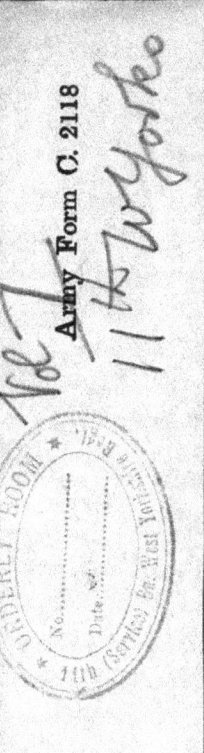

Army Form C. 2118

WAR DIARY
or
INTELLIGENCE SUMMARY
(Erase heading not required.)

Instructions regarding War Diaries and Intelligence Summaries are contained in F.S. Regs., Part II. and the Staff Manual respectively. Title Pages will be prepared in manuscript.

Place	Date	Hour	Summary of Events and Information	Remarks and references to Appendices
ERQUINGHEM	13.2.16		Billets	
	14.2.16		" marched from billets in RUE DORMOIRE to billets at VIEUX BERQUIN leaving at 10 p.m.	
	15.2.16		"	
VIEUX BERQUIN	16.2.16	4 a.m.	Arrived VIEUX BERQUIN.	
		9 a.m.	Left VIEUX BERQUIN	
		3 p.m.	Arrived STEENBECQUE in billets in III Corps Rest Area.	
	17.2.16		Rest Area Training	
	18.2.16		"	
	19.2.16		"	
	20.2.16		"	
	21.2.16		"	
	22.2.16		"	
ESTAIRES	23.2.16		marched to billets at ESTAIRES.	
	24.2.16		Billets	
	25.2.16		"	
	26.2.16		"	
			" marched back to billets at STEENBECQUE	
STEENBECQUE	27.2.16		Rest Area Training	
	28.2.16		" marched to STEENBECQUE Station & entrained	
	29.2.16	8 a.m.	Disembarked CALLONNE RICQUART marched to billets at HALLICOURT	
		11 a.m.	Arrived	

J.P. Bedwell Capt.
& Adjutant,
11th (Service) Bn. West Yorkshire Regt.

WAR DIARY or INTELLIGENCE SUMMARY

11th (Service) Bn. West Yorkshire Regt.

Place	Date	Hour	Summary of Events and Information	Remarks and references to Appendices
Hallecourt			MARCH, 1916.	
	1st		In Billets Training	
	2nd		do	
	3rd		do	
	4th		do	
	5th		do	
GRANDE SERVINS	6th		Marched to billets at GRANDE SERVINS.	
TRENCHES	7th		In the evening relieved French Regt in trenches in Right sub-section of the Souchez sector. Very slow relief owing to communication trenches inundated, trenches very bad, weather very wet. Night quiet.	
"	8.		Throughout the day the enemy bombarded our trenches & dugouts intermittently with Trench Mortars, whizzbangs & 5.9 shells doing very little material damage to wire, trenches & dugouts. high wet very quiet. Nothing to report on artillery reprisals.	
"	9.		The enemy fired Trench mortar bombs & also some aerial torpedos throughout the day. Enemy snipers more active, especially opposite our Right Company. Night very quiet.	
"	10.		The day passed quietly, very little shell or rifle fire. This Bn. was relieved by 2nd WORCESTERS in the evening & on relief marched out to billets at GRANDE SERVINS.	
GRANDE SERVINS	11th		Billets	
"	12th		"	

WAR DIARY
or
INTELLIGENCE SUMMARY
(Erase heading not required.)

Army Form C. 2118

Place	Date	Hour	Summary of Events and Information	Remarks and references to Appendices
GRANDE SERVINS	13th		March 1916. Marched to billets at Callonne Ricquart.	
CALLONNE RICQUART	14th		Billets. Training	
	15th		do	
	16th		do	
	17th		do	
	18th		Marched to billets at HERSIN.	
	19th		Relieved 17th Royal Fusiliers in trenches (Right B2 centre) Bos ANGRES Section). The night passed quietly practically no rifle fire the enemy fired a great number of coloured lights but not action.	
	20th		Day & night very quiet nothing to report	
	21st		At about 10 pm enemy fired about 4 rounds of shrapnel 17 bombs burst in the air Lord our Left Company. At 6.30 pm 6 rifle grenades were fired into the same place night very quiet.	
	22nd		The enemy shelled our support & communication trenches intermittently through out the day with 4.2 shells & shrapnel doing no material damage. About 25 rifle grenades were fired into our Left Company.	

1875. Wt. W593/826 1,000,000 4/15 J.B.C. & A. A.D.S.S./Forms/C. 2118.

12th (Service) Bn. West Yorkshire Regt.

WAR DIARY
or
INTELLIGENCE SUMMARY
(Erase heading not required.)

Army Form C. 2118

Place	Date	Hour	Summary of Events and Information	Remarks and references to Appendices
Trenches			March. 1916.	
	23rd		The enemy bombarded our front line trenches throughout the afternoon with Trench mortar bombs rifle grenades shrapnel & 77. m.m. shells & our supports with H.E shells & H.E. Shrapnel, our artillery retaliated whenever not silence the enemy. The night passed quietly.	
	24th	About 7.30 a.m.	T.M. bombs fell in our Right Company of Remainder of day & night enemy very quiet.	
	25th		Enemy very quiet nothing to report.	
	26th		Enemy very quiet about 20 rifle grenades were fired into our left Coy at 5.30 p.m, otherwise nothing to report.	
	27th		During afternoon enemy shelled our supports & fired rifle grenades into our front line, our artillery retaliated. There was a good deal of random rifle fire during the night.	
	28th	About 4.30 p.m.	Enemy quiet during the morning. at about the enemy shelled our right Coy with about 25. 77 m.m Shells & rifle grenade doing no material damage. Again in the afternoon about 5 pm the enemy period 15-rifle grenades fell on left Coy, our artillery retaliated and silenced the enemy.	

Army Form C. 2118

WAR DIARY
or
INTELLIGENCE SUMMARY
(Erase heading not required.)

Place	Date	Hour	Summary of Events and Information	Remarks and references to Appendices
Trenches	March 19			
	29th	5 pm	The enemy shelled our left-hand with 5.7" in shells killing Stromer wounding Threa, our men, we retaliated with 4 rounds T.M. ammn which all burst into the German front line. The Germans then sent between 20 to 30 4.2 shells into our support line doing considerable damage.	
	30th	3.40 pm	During the afternoon the enemy fired about 20 7" in shells on our left-hand, but no material damage was done.	
	31st	10.30 A.M.	The enemy shelled the communication trenches but no material damage was done.	

A Kybalchuz 2nd Lieut T. Adjt
1st / 7th B. Batt:
West Yorks. Regt.

G.H.Q.
A.G's Office
3rd Echelon
Rouen.

11 W Yorks
Vol 6

We herewith forward War Diary for the month of April 1916

Kindly acknowledge receipt hereon,

C W G Baldry 2nd Lt.
Acting Adjt.
11th Bn. West Yorks Regt.

2-5-16

ORDERLY ROOM
No............
Date............
11th (Service) Bn. West Yorkshire Regt.

WAR DIARY or INTELLIGENCE SUMMARY

Army Form C. 2118

Place	Date	Hour	Summary of Events and Information	Remarks and references to Appendices
Trenches	1-4-16 2-4-16		Enemy very quiet. Nothing to report. The enemy threw over a large number of rifle grenades during the day but no material damage was done except one man killed and 2 men wounded. The night was quiet until midnight when some red flares were sent up on our right about a mile away, firing opened gun & rifle action continued for about an hour.	
	3-4-16		One of our patrols went out from our left sap to gain the German wire. They returned at 11-15 p.m. and reported large German working parties in both ends of the left sap. The patrol was quiet on several times. M. Gun opened fire on the German working party but were unable to touch them on account of the mounds as nomans land. Nothing else of importance happened.	
	4-4-16		During the day the enemy were very quiet. At 3-15 about 20 shrapnel shells were fired into our front line. Little damage was done. A quiet night. At 7-15 p.m. an officers patrol went out & found nothing of importance. Again at 2-15 a.m. an Officers patrol went out & returned at 3 a.m. & reported working party out again. The working party were fired on by our Artillery and would not work up to 5½ an hour.	
	5-4-16		Enemy very quiet during the day. Between 5-6 p.m. several rifle grenades were fired into our left bay, but no material damage was done. A few rifle grenades and shrapnel into our Rt & line R.O.D. the day very quiet. About midnight several lights were sent up on our right, but no artillery action took place.	
	6-4-16		Our Snipers claimed 2 of the enemy during the day. Our Artillery carried out a preparaged barrage fire on the German supporting trenches. Enemy fairly quiet during the night.	
	6-4-16		Enemy very quiet during the day except for a few rifle grenades. About 9.35 p.m. the enemy burst a red flare on their parapet in front of our right bay, their machine gun was very active & traversed our parapet. Later during the night. At 2.30 a.m. the enemy fired a green light at 3.30 a.m. a red one.	

Army Form C. 2118

Instructions regarding War Diaries and Intelligence Summaries are contained in F.S. Regs., Part II. and the Staff Manual respectively. Title Pages will be prepared in manuscript.

WAR DIARY or INTELLIGENCE SUMMARY

(Erase heading not required.)

Place	Date	Hour	Summary of Events and Information	Remarks and references to Appendices
Trenches	9-4-16		Very quiet during the day. One of our snipers claims to have hit a German. About 9 pm last night a good many lid flares were put up on our left. Artillery action took place and shelling lasted for about ½ hour. Then several Very flares were sent from our lines up. The action also took place about 1 mile away. During the rest of the night there was a great deal of machine gun and rifle fire. Nothing unusual.	
	10-4-16		During the day a good many rifle grenades were fired into our trenches. But no material damage was done. We retaliated with trench mortars. Trench mortars fired at ours behind the German lines during the night. Between 9 pm and midnight one of our patrols reported a German working party out in front of their front line. We gave a few bursts of machine gun fire in the direction of the party and work ceased.	
	11-4-16		Very quiet during the day. At 9 pm a German aeroplane was seen coming from the direction of the German lines and passed over head. At 9-40 pm it returned & dropped three Very lights. She went from the German lines. About 2 minutes later 2 more green lights were dropped; a swift red stationary light appeared in upper air. About 11-30 pm an engine whistle was heard behind enemy lines, otherwise the night was quiet.	
	12-4-16		One of our snipers claims to have hit a German. Large German working parties have again been seen on about M 26 & B 3. Our artillery opened fire but work only ceased for about ½ hour. Nothing else of importance to report.	

WAR DIARY or INTELLIGENCE SUMMARY

Army Form C. 2118

Place	Date	Hour	Summary of Events and Information	Remarks and references to Appendices
Trenches	13-4-16		Enemy very quiet during day and night. A few rifle grenades exchanged during the day. Nothing else of importance happened.	
	14-4-16		Early during the morning the enemy fired several rifle grenades and again after dark. One man wounded.	
			Our snipers claim to have hit a German, rather more sniping & machine gun fire during the night otherwise the enemy were exceptionally quiet.	
	15-4-16		B.H.Q. moved to H.Q. in Machine Shed. Coy in reserve move into front line. Relieved a Coy & half of the West Riding Regt. Every very quiet.	
	16-4-16		Battn. relieved on the night of 16 & 17 by the 17th R. Fusiliers being very active during day & night. The Battn. now billeted in billets at zone 12.	
	17-4-16		Marched from zone 10 to DIVION.	
	18-4-16		Remained at DIVION.	
Billets	19-4-16		Marched to MATRINGHEM. Manoeuvring Area.	
	20-4-16		Cleaning up.	
	21-4-16		Battalion training.	
	22-4-16		Brigade training.	
	23-4-16		Battalion training during the morning. Light operations in the morning training afternoon.	
	24-4-16		Marched to FIEFS & billeted for one night.	
	25-4-16		Marched to TURNES & entrained to d. 12.30pm for BARLIN. Marched from BARLIN to COUPIGNY where Batt. is billeted for digging area.	
	26-4-16		Cleaning up of camp & Battn parade.	
	27-4-16			

WAR DIARY or INTELLIGENCE SUMMARY

Place	Date	Hour	Summary of Events and Information	Remarks and references to Appendices
Billets BOUVIGNY	28-4-16		Batts. supplied digging parties for Bully, Bouvigny, Souchez Sector.	
	29-4-16		Church parade. Batt. inspection & cleaning up of camp.	
	30-4-16		Church parade, Inspection. Issuing pay & warrant for night 30/6-1/7	

Signed 2nd Lieut & act adjt
11" S. Batt. Worc. for the Bgh.
30-4-16

WAR DIARY or INTELLIGENCE SUMMARY

Army Form C. 2118

Place	Date	Hour	Summary of Events and Information	Remarks and references to Appendices
LOUPIGNY	1-5-16		Billets	
"	2-5-16		G.O.C. Bde. Inspection.	
"	3-5-16		"	
"	4-5-16		"	
DIVION	5-5-16		Marched to Divion & took over billets from the 2nd Royal Fusiliers. Foot lame. The Batt attended a gas demonstration in the afternoon.	
"	6-5-16		G.O.C's Bde Inspection.	
"	7-5-16		Division.	
"	8-5-16		"	
"	9-5-16		"	
"	10-5-16		Marched to FOSSE 10 & relieved the 2td R. Fusiliers.	
"	11-5-16		Billets	
"	12-5-16		"	
"	13-5-16		"	
"	14-5-16		"	
"	15-5-16		"	
"	16-5-16		"	
"	17-5-16		Relieved the 10 West Riding in the Angres Section.	
"	18-5-16		Trenches. Enemy rather active with Trench Mortars & 4.2 shell.	
	19/5/16		Trenches. Enemy very active during the morning with rifle grenades we retaliated with Trench Mortars & considerably silenced the enemy nothing else to report.	
	20/5/16		Trenches quiet day nothing unusual to report.	
	21/5/16		Trenches, morning quiet, during the afternoon the enemy bombarded our trenches heavily with 75mm shells & fashing atory shells, in consequence of which a few S.O.S. was received from the night, the shelling continued intermittently until 9.30 pm no material damage was done.	

WAR DIARY or INTELLIGENCE SUMMARY

Army Form C. 2118

Place	Date	Hour	Summary of Events and Information	Remarks and references to Appendices
	22/5/16		Trenches, morning quiet. Enemy shelled slightly in about 1/2 hour during the afternoon. Relieved by 10th West Riding Regt in evening.	
	23/5/16 24/5/16 25/5/16 26/5/16		Billets Bully Grenay. do do do	
			relieved 10th West Riding in the trenches in evening. Night quiet.	
	27/5/16		Day very quiet on our front, considerable bombardment of our trenches on our left occurred during the night.	
	28/5/16		Enemy snipers & trench mortars active all day to which we retaliated. Night very quiet.	
	29/5/16		Day very quiet, nothing unusual to report.	
	30/5/16		Trench mortar activity on both sides during the morning enemy eventually silenced. Relieved by 2nd Northamptonshire Regt in the evening.	
	31/5/16		Billets in FOSSE TEN near HERSIN.	

J.F. Bedwell
Capt & Adjutant
11th (Service) Bn. West Yorkshire Regt

WAR DIARY or INTELLIGENCE SUMMARY

Army Form C.2118

11 West Yorks Vol 8

XXIII

Place	Date	Hour	Summary of Events and Information	Remarks and references to Appendices
FOSSE 10.	June 1-1916		Billets - training.	
"	2/6/16		" "	
"	3/6/16		" "	
"	4/6/16		" "	
"	5/6/16		" "	
"	6/6/16		" "	
"	7/6/16		" "	
"	8/6/16		" "	
BOIS DE NOULETTE	9/6/16		Relieved 10th Northumberland Fusiliers in huts at BOIS DE NOULETTE.	
"	10/6/16		Training & working parties.	
"	11/6/16		" "	
"	12/6/16		" "	
"	13/6/16		Relieved by 140th Brigade marched to Bethune VEDREL	
VEDREL.	14/6/16		Left VEDREL and marched to CALONNE RICOUART.	
CALONNE-RICOUART	15/6/16		Cleaning harness.	
ENQUIN-LES-MINES	16/6/16		Marched to billets at ENQUIN-LES-MINES.	
"	17/6/16		Brigade manoeuvres	
"	18/6/16		Training.	
"	19/6/16		Divisional manoeuvres	
"	20/6/16		Battalion training	
"	21/6/16		"	
"	22/6/16		"	
"	23/6/16		"	
"	24/6 & 25/6		Marched to BERGUETTE and entrained for at 9.10 p.m. arrived at LONGUEAU at 5.30 a.m. 25th June & marched to billets at ST. VAST-AU-CHAUSSEE arrived at 12.45 p.m.	

WAR DIARY
or
INTELLIGENCE SUMMARY

(Erase heading not required.)

Army Form C. 2118

Instructions regarding War Diaries and Intelligence Summaries are contained in F. S. Regs., Part II. and the Staff Manual respectively. Title Pages will be prepared in manuscript.

Place	Date	Hour	Summary of Events and Information	Remarks and references to Appendices
ST. VAAST-AU-CHAUSSÉE	26/6/16		Billets cleaning parades.	
-"-	27/6		-"-	
-"-	28/6		Ordered to move - cancelled - Battalion ordered to clean feet.	
-"-	29/6		Brigade route march.	
-"-	30/6		Left ST. VAAST-AU-CHAUSSÉE and marched to COISEY arriving at 6.30 p.m.	

J C Pearson 2/Lt
a/Adjt
1/4th (S) W Yorks Regt

69th Inf.Bde.
23rd Div.

11th BATTN. THE WEST YORKSHIRE REGIMENT.

J U L Y

1 9 1 6

11 W Yorks
Vol 9

INTELLIGENCE SUMMARY
(Erase heading not required.)

Place	Date July	Hour	Summary of Events and Information	Remarks and references to Appendices
COISY	1st		Left COISY at 8 p.m. marched to billets at BAZIEUX.	
BAZIEUX	2nd		Left BAZIEUX & bivouacked outside ALBERT.	
ALBERT	3rd		Left bivouac & marched to BECOURT WOOD. Relieved 16th Royal Scots Regt. in trenches at SCOTS REDOUBT at 11.30 p.m.	
SCOTS REDOUBT	4th		Attacked the enemy lines during the afternoon & obtained our objective. We were forced to retire & fell back on our own lines.	
"	5th	12.15	Again attacked enemy position & were in it for a time, but were again forced to retire owing to a strong counter-attack. At 3.30 the Regiment, with the 9th Yorks. Regt. to West & Lincoln Regt. again attacked the German trenches & captured the position & retained about 300 prisoners. We were relieved by the 8th Yorkshire Regt. at 10 p.m. & bivouacked near BECOURT WOOD.	
BECOURT WOOD	6th		The Battn. bivouaced near E10D.	
ON THE MARCH	7th		Moved back to BECOURT WOOD where temporarily attached to the 2nd Brigade. Bivouaced at FRICOURT FARM.	
"	8th		Moved back to BECOURT WOOD. At 6 p.m. marched to billets in ALBERT.	
ALBERT	9th		Battn. in billets - cleaning parades.	
TRENCHES	10th		Relieved the 6th Brigade in trenches near CONTALMAISON. At 11.30 p.m. the Battn. with the other units of the Brigade attacked and captured CONTALMAISON. The village was held & position consolidated. Lost 16 officers in this & the assault on 4th/5th inst. and about 350 men. The Battn. was relieved by the 10th Batt: Cameron Highlanders at 11.15 p.m. & marched to billets at ALBERT.	
ALBERT	11th		Battn. resting & cleaning.	
ON THE MARCH	12th		Marched to FRANVILLERS. In billets.	
"	13th		Left FRANVILLERS & marched to billets in MOLLIENS-AU-BOIS	

INTELLIGENCE SUMMARY

(Erase heading not required.)

Instructions regarding War Diaries and Intelligence Summaries are contained in F.S. Regs., Part II. and the Staff Manual respectively. Title Pages will be prepared in manuscript.

Place	Date July.	Hour	Summary of Events and Information	Remarks and references to Appendices
MOLLIEN-AU-BOIS	14th		In billets at MOLLIENS-AU-BOIS. Cleaning parade. Inspected by G.O.C. Division at 6 p.m.	
"	15th		In billets. Inspected by 3rd. CORPS Commander at 10 a.m.	
"	16		In billets. Battalion drill	
"	17th		"	
"	18th		" Working parades.	
"	19th		"	
"	20th		Battalion training. Lecture to officers mess by Corps Chemist on gas-shells.	
ON THE MARCH	21		Battalion drill & kit inspection.	
MILLENCOURT	22nd		Marched to MILLENCOURT, arriving at 2.16 p.m.	
"	23rd		In billets. Company training.	
"	24th		Battalion drill. Under 1 hr. notice to move after midnight.	
"	25th		" ½ hr. notice cancelled	
"	26		"	
TRENCHES	27th		Left MILLENCOURT & relieved the Royal Sussex Regt. in Old British line Nr. near BECOURT WOOD.	
"	28th		Cleaning trenches & building & repairing dug-outs & shelters.	
CONTALMAISON	29th		Relieved the 13th Batt. D.L.I. in CONTALMAISON. Enemy shelling heavily.	
"	30th		In CONTALMAISON. Enemy shelling heavily.	
"	31st		" "	* Enemy using new gas shells. No casualties from gas poisoning, but gas hung about ‡ * trench. ‡ awkward when gas poisonous but no slightly gassed.

J.E. Pitman 2/L + Act/Adjt.
11 (S) Batt. West Yorkshire Regt.

22.
SB
EB

2/   69th Brigade.
     23rd Division

1/11th BATTALION

           WEST YORKSHIRE REGIMENT

                      AUGUST 1 9 1 6

Army Form C. 2118.

WAR DIARY
or
INTELLIGENCE SUMMARY.
(Erase heading not required.)

11. W. Yorks Vol 10

Instructions regarding War Diaries and Intelligence Summaries are contained in F.S. Regs., Part II. and the Staff Manual respectively. Title pages will be prepared in manuscript.

Place	Date	Hour	Summary of Events and Information	Remarks and references to Appendices
ALBERT.	Aug 1st		In CONTALMAISON. relieved by 10th Northumberland Fusiliers. moved to billets in ALBERT.	
"	2		Battalion in billets in ALBERT. Cleaning up Parades.	
"	3		" " Parties (parades).	
"	4		" "	
CONTALMAISON.	5		Battalion left billets in ALBERT at 2 p.m. & proceeded to CONTALMAISON, relieving 10th North? Fus: in CONTALMAISON.	
"	6			
"	7		Bath. in CONTALMAISON. 2½ Companies in Front line trenches, H.Q. Bomber's road in rear of station Venolia alley.	
BRESLE.	8		Battalion march from CONTALMAISON to BRESLE. Relieved by the 5th Inf Brigade.	
"	9		In billets at BRESLE. Cleaning parades.	
"	10		" "	
"	11		Entrained at MERICOURT at 12.30 am. for BELLACOURT arrived in billets at 12 noon.	
BELLACOURT	12		In billets at BELLANCOURT. Cleaning parades.	
"	13		Entrained at 11.35 pm for BAILLEUL.	
ON THE MARCH	14		Arrived at BAILLEUL 9.30 am - marched to billets at MOUNT KOKEREELE.	
MOUNT KOKEREELE	15		In billets at MOUNT KOKEREELE. Kit inspection.	

23.
8/3

Army Form C. 2118.

WAR DIARY
or
INTELLIGENCE SUMMARY.
(Erase heading not required.)

Instructions regarding War Diaries and Intelligence
Summaries are contained in F. S. Regs., Part II.
and the Staff Manual respectively. Title pages
will be prepared in manuscript.

Place	Date	Hour	Summary of Events and Information	Remarks and references to Appendices
MOUNT KOKEREELE	Aug 16		In billets at Mount Kokereele. Battalion parade full marching order inspection.	
"	17		Marched from MOUNT KOKEREELE to proceed to billets in STEEN WERCK AREA.	
STEEN WERCK	18		Marched to billets in ROMARIN near NIEPPE.	
ROMARIN	19		In billets at PAPOT, ROMARIN.	
"	20		"	
"	21		"	
CRESLOW	22		Moved to reserve position in CRESLOW.	
"	23		In CRESLOW. Working parties found.	
"	24		"	
"	25		Left CRESLOW for LEWISHAM LODGE. Battalion in immediate support to front line. Working parties found.	24/8
LEWISHAM LODGE	26		LEWISHAM LODGE - working parties found.	
"	27		"	
"	28		"	
"	29		"	
"	30		"	
"	31		"	

R Pitman
2/Lt
& Adjutant,
11th (Service) Bn. West Yorkshire Regt.

WAR DIARY or INTELLIGENCE SUMMARY

Army Form C. 2118

23/69 Vol II

Place	Date	Hour	Summary of Events and Information	Remarks and references to Appendices
	Sept 1 1916		Battalion in Reserve Billets LEWISHAM LODGE, PLUGSTEERT. Working Parties.	
"	-2		Moved to HOPE STREET. Relieved 10th West Ridings in front line. Enemy made Gas attack on our left and shelled our front line trenches. Casualties 3 killed and 1 wounded.	
"	-3		In trenches HOPE STREET. Quiet all day.	
"	-4		Relieved by 7th Bn. Loyal North Lancs Regt. Marched to Burracks at S.27 near BAILLEUL.	
"	-5		In trenches at S.27 BAILLEUL.	
"	-6		Entrained at BAILLEUL for ST. OMER and thence marched to Billets at EPERLECQUES.	
"	-7		In Billets at EPERLECQUES. Brigade Training.	
"	-8		do do	
"	-9		do do	
"	-10		Marched to AUDRICQUE Station and entrained for LONGEAU.	
"	-11		Arrived at LONGEAU and marched to COISY.	
"	-12		Marched to Billets in HENNENCOURT WOOD	
"	-13		In Billets do do Physical Training Coy and Battalion drills.	
"	-14		do do	
"	-15		Marched to Billets at MILLENCOURT.	

Army Form C. 2118

WAR DIARY
or
INTELLIGENCE SUMMARY
(Erase heading not required.)

Instructions regarding War Diaries and Intelligence Summaries are contained in F.S. Regs., Part II. and the Staff Manual respectively. Title Pages will be prepared in manuscript.

Place	Date 1916	Hour	Summary of Events and Information	Remarks and references to Appendices
	Sept 16		Battalion in Billets at MILLENCOURT. Battalion Training.	
	- 17		Do Do	
	- 18		Moved to MARTINPUICH and relieved 46th Brigade.	
	- 19		In trenches PUSH ALLEY - GUNPIT ROAD - and FACTORY LINE, MARTINPUICH.	
	- 20		Do Do	
	- 21		Do Do	
	- 22		Marched to Bivouacs at WILLOW PATCH, near ROUND WOOD.	
	- 23		In Bivouacs near ROUND WOOD. Working parties.	
	- 24		Do do	
	- 25		Do do	
	- 26		Took over GOURLAY Support trenches, working parties.	
	- 27		In GOURLAY Support trenches, working parties.	
	- 28		Do do	
	- 29		Do do	
	- 30		Do do	

Ashmonde
for Officer Commanding
11th (Service) Bn. West Yorkshire Regt.

Army Form C. 2118.

11 West Yorks

WAR DIARY
or
INTELLIGENCE SUMMARY.
(Erase heading not required.)

Vol 12

Instructions regarding War Diaries and Intelligence Summaries are contained in F. S. Regs., Part II and the Staff Manual respectively. Title pages will be prepared in manuscript.

Place	Date 1916	Hour	Summary of Events and Information	Remarks and references to Appendices
MARTINPUICH	1st	6 a.m	Moved to trenches near MARTIN PUICH	
"	2nd		Trenches MARTINPUICH	
"	3rd		—	
"	4th		—	
Trenches near LE SARS	5th		Battn moved up towards LE SARS (Newfoundland to 26th Avenue)	
"	6th		Trenches – about 26th Avenue	
"	7th	2.10 pm	Battn attacked German F.L. left of LE SARS. Objective gained H.O.P. loss heavy. 80 officers & 217 O.R.	
LE SARS	8th		Battn. relieved by 6th Camerons, 147th Brigade 4th Division bivouaced in ROUND WOOD	
ROUND WOOD	9th		Battn. left ROUND WOOD bivouaced in billets in ALBERT.	
ALBERT	10th		Billets in ALBERT. Day spent in cleaning up & equipment. Drawing new clothes & issue where necessary.	
"	11th		Billets in ALBERT. Battn paraded & inspected by Corps Commander. Battalion parades.	
"	12th	10 pm	Entrained at ALBERT for LONGPRÉ.	
LONGPRÉ	13th		Detrained at LONGPRÉ at 4 am & immediately broke from thence station to COULONVILLIERS arriving at 10.20 am	
On the March	14th		Entrained at CONTEVILLE at 11 am for HOUPOUTRE station, BELGIUM	
"	15th		Arrived at HOUPOUTRE Station at 6 am & marched to billets in POPERINGHE	
POPERINGHE	16th		In billets. Day spent in cleaning up & platoon drill	

2353 Wt. W.25141/1454 700,000 5/15 D.D.&L. A.D.S.S./Forms/C.2118.

Army Form C. 2118.

WAR DIARY
or
INTELLIGENCE SUMMARY.
(Erase heading not required.)

Instructions regarding War Diaries and Intelligence Summaries are contained in F. S. Regs., Part II. and the Staff Manual respectively. Title pages will be prepared in manuscript.

Place	Date	Hour	Summary of Events and Information	Remarks and references to Appendices
	Oct.			
POPERINGHE	17th		In billets. Platoon Company drill.	
"	18th		" Route march.	
"	19th		" Company drill, training parades.	
"	20th		" "	
"	21st		Company drill. Company up parades.	
"	22nd		In billets preparing to move to YPRES.	
YPRES	23rd		Batt: billets in Infantry Barracks. Working parties for front-line system found.	
"	24th		" "	
"	25th		" " Commdg off. new on have. Capt N. Crosbie in command.	
"	26th		" " Transport-officer on leave.	
"	27th		" "	
"	28th		" "	
TRENCHES	29th		Batt. relieves the 10th WEST RIDING REGT in the front-line system. Relief complete by 11.45 p.m.	
"	30th		In trenches. Situation quiet.	
"	31st		" Enemy made a bombing attack on our forward posts causing 5 casualties. The post was retaken & again occupied without further casualties.	

2353 Wt. W3544/1454 700,000 5/15 D. D. & L. A.D.S.S./Forms/C. 2118.

Army Form C. 2118.

11th W. Bat Yorkshire Regt.

Vol 13

WAR DIARY
or
INTELLIGENCE SUMMARY.
(Erase heading not required.)

Instructions regarding War Diaries and Intelligence Summaries are contained in F. S. Regs., Part II and the Staff Manual respectively. Title pages will be prepared in manuscript.

Place	Date	Hour	Summary of Events and Information	Remarks and references to Appendices
TRENCHES IN YPRES SALIENT	1916 Nov 1		Batt. in trenches - day quiet	
"	2		"	
"	3		"	
"	4		Battn. relieved by 5th Yorks Lanc: Regt. march to barracks in YPRES. ST LAWRENCE CAMP, near POPERINGHE.	
ST LAWRENCE CAMP	5		arrived at ST LAWRENCE CAMP at 2 am	
"	6		day about in cleaning up.	
"	7		Battn. parade, foundation Drill & G.O.C. Division.	
"	8		Battn. Comp. training	
"	9		"	
"	10		Entrained for Infantry barracks YPRES unreaded C. ZILLE BEEKE BUND. relieved 18th Durham Lgt. Inft.	
ZILLEBEEKE BUND	11		Batt. Working parties	
"	12		"	
"	13		"	
"	14		"	
"	15		"	
"	16		Party parade, Batt. move up to front-line relieved 10th Duke of Wellingtons Regt. M.O. DORMY HOUSE	

Army Form C. 2118.

WAR DIARY
or
INTELLIGENCE SUMMARY.

(Erase heading not required.)

Instructions regarding War Diaries and Intelligence
Summaries are contained in F.S. Regs., Part II.
and the Staff Manual respectively. Title pages
will be prepared in manuscript.

Place	Date	Hour	Summary of Events and Information	Remarks and references to Appendices
	1916			
TRENCHES FRONT LINE	18		Spent in trenches - decorator quiet.	
"	19		" " "	
"	20		" " - Slight enemy aviation activity by enemy	
"	21		" " - Bombing attack carried out by 10" New-Intry bt - our casualties 2 killed 1 wounded	
"	22		" " - Situation quiet - very much as day.	
ST LAWRENCE	23		Relieved by 5th K.O.Y.L.I. entrained at YPRES for ST LAWRENCE CAMP.	
CAMP.	24		Battn. arrived at ST LAWRENCE CAMP at 1.30 a.m.	
"	25		Battn. in ST LAWRENCE CAMP. Cleaning up parades	
"	26		" " "	
"	27		" " Coy drill	
"	28		" " Church parade.	
"	29		" " C.O. inspects new drafts; working parties.	
YPRES	29		Relieved 10th Northumberland Fusiliers in Infantry Barracks YPRES.	
	30		Batts. on working parties. Coy drill inoculation carried out.	

J.R. Purvis
Lt Col. ??? Bn.
OC. 11 West Yorks Bn.

Army Form C. 2118.

WAR DIARY
or
INTELLIGENCE SUMMARY.
(Erase heading not required.)

11th W. Yorks.   Vol 14

Place	Date	Hour	Summary of Events and Information	Remarks and references to Appendices
	Dec			
YPRES	1st		Batt. in Infantry Barracks in YPRES. Cleaning up & working parties.	
	2nd		— do —	
	3rd		— do — Working parties attend Parade.	
TRENCHES	4th		Batt. in the line. Day quiet except for occasional small shells. Relieved 10" D of Wellington Regt in front line trenches.	
"	5th		— do — Situation normal. Enemy shelled front line intermittently. Wiring parties out on MENIN ROAD.	
"	6		— do — Situation normal. Relieved by 10" D of Wellington Regt. — do —	
YPRES	7th		Batt. in billets in Infantry Barracks. Working parties.	
"	8th		— do —	
"	9th		— do —	
"	10th		— do —	
"	11"		Batt. relieved 10" Duke of Wellington Regt in front line.	
TRENCHES	12th		Batt. in the line. Situation quiet all day. Wiring parties & patrols out.	
"	13th		— do —	
"	14th		— do —	
"	15th		Batt. relieved by 8th Batt. York Lancs. & proceeded to ST LAWRENCE CAMP. No casualties during 16 days tour.	
ST LAWRENCE CAMP	16th		Arrived in ST LAWRENCE CAMP about 1 a.m. Cleaning & parade inspection.	

Army Form C. 2118.

WAR DIARY
or
INTELLIGENCE SUMMARY.
(Erase heading not required.)

Instructions regarding War Diaries and Intelligence Summaries are contained in F.S. Regs., Part II. and the Staff Manual respectively. Title pages will be prepared in manuscript.

Place	Date	Hour	Summary of Events and Information	Remarks and references to Appendices
	Dec.			
ST LAWRENCE CAMP.	17th		Battn: training. Church parade. Working parties.	
"	18th		Inspection. Cleaning up parades.	
"	19th		Working parties. Company drill.	
"	20th		"	
"	21st		Battn: rest day for purpose of Christmas dinner to men.	
"	22nd		Battn: training. Coy. + platoon drill.	
"	23rd		Relieved 10th Northumberland Fusiliers - Hospice at YPRES.	
YPRES.	24th		Church parade. Working parties all day.	
"	25th		Church services. Working parties all day. Enemy shelled YPRES square with 4.2 during afternoon.	
"	26th		Battn: on working parties all day.	
"	27th		Battn: relieved 10th Duke of Wellington Regt: in support sector of Brigade Front.	
TRENCHES	28th		Battn: in line. Day quiet except for few enemy trench mortars. 1 casualty.	
"	29th		—do.— Enemy trench mortars front line fairly heavily. Our artillery retaliates	
"	30th		—do.—	
"	31st		Battn: relieved by 10th Bde of Wellington Regt: Arrived at Hospice about 9:30 p.m. Enemy shelled front line during afternoon.	

W.P. Stuart Gray
Lt. Adj.
11th West Yorkshire Regt.

Army Form C. 2118.

WAR DIARY
or
INTELLIGENCE SUMMARY.
(Erase heading not required.)

Instructions regarding War Diaries and Intelligence Summaries are contained in F. S. Regs., Part II. and the Staff Manual respectively. Title pages will be prepared in manuscript.

Place	Date	Hour	Summary of Events and Information	Remarks and references to Appendices
YPRES	Dec. 1st		Battn. in Killed = Infantry Barracks = YPRES. Cleaning up & working parties.	
	2nd		— do —	
	3rd		(")	
TRENCHES	4th		Working parties nightly. Reveues. Relieved 10" Duke of Wellington Regt. in front line trenches	
	5th		Battn. in the front line. Quiet except for occasional enemy shells. Wiring parties out on MENIN ROAD.	
	6th		— do — Situation normal. Enemy shelled front line intermittently. Wiring parties out on whole front.	
			— do — Situation normal. Relieved by 10" Duke of Wellington Regt.	— do —
YPRES	7th		Battn. in Killed in Infantry Barracks. Working parties.	
	8th		— do —	
	9th		— do —	
	10th		— do —	
	11th		Battn. relieved 10" Duke of Wellington Regt. in front line.	
TRENCHES	12th		Battn. in the line. Situation quiet all day. Wiring parties posted out.	
	13th		— do —	
	14th		— do —	
	15th		Battn. relieved by 9R Batn. York Lancs. & proceeded to ST LAWRENCE CAMP. No casualties during 16 days tour.	
ST LAWRENCE CAMP	16th		Proceeded to ST LAWRENCE CAMP about 2am. Having to attend inspection.	

Army Form C. 2118.

WAR DIARY
or
INTELLIGENCE SUMMARY.
(Erase heading not required.)

Instructions regarding War Diaries and Intelligence Summaries are contained in F. S. Regs., Part II. and the Staff Manual respectively. Title pages will be prepared in manuscript.

Place	Date	Hour	Summary of Events and Information	Remarks and references to Appendices
	Dec.			
AN AINCE CAMP.	17th		Battn: traing. church parade – Working parties	
"	18th		Snowstorm. Mending up bivouacs.	
"	19th		Working parties & company drill.	
"	20th		"	
"	21st		Battn: rest day for purpose of Christmas dinner to men.	
"	22nd		Battn: traing. Coy. + platoon drill.	
"	23rd		Relieved 10th Northumberland Fusiliers in Hoobie at YPRES.	
YPRES.	24th		Church parade. Working parties all day.	
"	25th		Church service. Working parties all day. Enemy shells YPRES square with H.E. during the afternoon.	
"	26th		Battn. on working parties all day.	
"	27th		Battn: relieved 10th Duke of Wellington Regt. in near sector of Brigade front.	
TRENCHES	28th		Battn. in line. Day quiet except for few enemy trench mortars. 1 Casualty.	
"	29th		do – Enemy trench mortars front line fairly heavily. Our artillery retaliate	
"	30th		– do –	
"	31st		Battn. relieved by 10th Bn. Duke of Wellington Regt. Arrived at Hoobie about 7.30 p.m. Enemy shelled front line during afternoon.	

M. P. Grant Major
O/C 11 West Yorkshire Regt.

Army Form C. 2118.

WAR DIARY
or
INTELLIGENCE SUMMARY.
(Erase heading not required.)

11th [Prince Albert's] Yorkshire Regt

Vol/5

Instructions regarding War Diaries and Intelligence Summaries are contained in F.S. Regs., Part II. and the Staff Manual respectively. Title pages will be prepared in manuscript.

Place	Date	Hour	Summary of Events and Information	Remarks and references to Appendices
YPRES	Jan 1917 1.		Battalion in Hopies. Working parties found daily	
"	2		Battn. furnish forestry, working parties found	
"	3		Battn. in Hopies. Working parties found	
"	4		Battn. relieved 10th West Riding Regt. in Left Batt. front of Right Sector. H.Q. Rudkin House	
TRENCHES	5		Battn. in front line trenches. Enemy trench mortars very active	
"	6		Trench Mortars active of both sides active	
"	7			
"	8.		Enemy action. YPRES - ZILLEBEKE shelled	
ST LAWRENCE	9		Battn relieved by 11 SHERWOOD FORESTERS. Arrived in ST LAWRENCE CAMP about 10.30 pm. Enemy active all day.	
CAMP	10		Battn in camp. Cleaning parade	
"	11		" " Scheme of work carried out. Coy Malim training.	
"	12		Battn. Scheme of work carried out. Working parties found	
"	13		" " " "	
"	14		" " " "	
"	15		" " " "	
TRENCHES	16		Batt. relieved 11th Bn. Northumberland Fusiliers in front line. H.Q. TUILLERIES. Enemy quiet	

Army Form C. 2118.

WAR DIARY
or
INTELLIGENCE SUMMARY.
(Erase heading not required.)

1/11 Bn West Yorkshire Regt

Instructions regarding War Diaries and Intelligence Summaries are contained in F. S. Regs., Part II. and the Staff Manual respectively. Title pages will be prepared in manuscript.

Place	Date	Hour	Summary of Events and Information	Remarks and references to Appendices
TRENCHES	Jan 1917 17		Batt. in front line. Slight artillery activity in afternoon.	
"	18		Enemy snipers active. Slight artillery activity. 1 Sgt. killed	
"	19		"	
"	20		Batt. relieved by 10 West Riding Regt. Batt. arrived at Infantry Barracks YPRES about 9 p.m.	
YPRES	21		Church relieving parade carried out.	
"	22		Batt. in Barracks. Cleaning parades working parties	
"	23		Batt. bathing parade, working parties found in morning only.	
"	24		Batt. relieved 10 West Riding Regt in front line. R.O.R. TUNNELLERS.	
TRENCHES	25		Day quiet. Trenches repairs during relieve carried out.	
"	26		"	
"	27		"	
"	28		Batt. relieved by 10 West Riding Regt arrived at Infantry Barracks YPRES arriving about 10 p.m. No casualties during tour.	
YPRES	29		Church cleaning parade & working parties	
"	30		Cleaning, football, drill, arms drill & working parties carried out. Day quiet.	B Spearman Lt Col 11 West Yorkshire Regt
"	31		Working parties found, cleaning scheme carried out. Day quiet.	

Army Form C. 2118.

WAR DIARY
~~INTELLIGENCE SUMMARY.~~
(Erase heading not required.)

11th Bn West Yorkshire Regt

Instructions regarding War Diaries and Intelligence Summaries are contained in F. S. Regs., Part II. and the Staff Manual respectively. Title pages will be prepared in manuscript.

Place	Date	Hour	Summary of Events and Information	Remarks and references to Appendices
YPRES	Jan 1917 1		Battalion in Hopper. Enemy posts found nearby	
	2		Battn. pushing forward. No enemy posts found.	
	3		Batt. in Hopper. Enemy posts found	
	4		Batt. relieved 10 West Riding Regt in 1st Batt. front. B. Right-Sector. N.A. Russian trench	
TRENCHES	5		Battn. in front line trenches. Enemy trench mortars very active.	
	6		Trench mortar active & 6pdr also active	
	7		Enemy active. YPRES TRENCHES SHELLED	
	8		Batt. relieved by 11 SHERWOOD FORESTERS (novel) — Stretcher camp about 0.30 pm being active all day.	
BIVOUACS	9		Batt in camp. Cleaning parade	
CAMP	10		" Cleaning work carried out, by platoon training.	
	11		Batt. cleaning & work carried out. Working parties found	
	12		"	
	13		"	
	14			
	15			
TRENCHES.	16		Batt. relieved 6th Northumberland Fusiliers in front line. SPO TRILLIERIES. Enemy quiet.	

WAR DIARY
or
INTELLIGENCE SUMMARY.
(Erase heading not required.)

Army Form C. 2118.

1/4th West Yorks R.

Place	Date	Hour	Summary of Events and Information	Remarks and references to Appendices
TRENCHES	Jan 1917 17		Battn in front line. Slight artillery action, in afternoon.	
"	18		Enemy airplane active. Slight artillery activity.	
"	19		1 Sgt killed	
"	20		Battn relieved by 10 West Riding Regt. Battn arrived at Infantry Barracks YPRES about 9 pm.	
YPRES	21		Church parades. Carried out.	
"	22		Battn in Barracks. Cleaning parades, working parties.	
"	23		Batt. bathing parade. Working parties found in morning only.	
"	24		Battn relieved 10" West Riding Regt in front line. R.Q. TURCOING.	
TRENCHES	25		Day quiet. Trenches & parapets during extreme carried out.	
"	26			
"	27			
"	28		Batt. relieved by 10' West Riding Regt. arrived at Infantry Barracks YPRES arriving about 10 pm. No casualties during tour.	
YPRES	29		Whole cleaning parades & working parties.	
"	30		Cleaning, gas helmet drill, arm drill, recreating parties carried out. Day quiet.	
"	31		Working parties found, wiring, relieve carried out. Day quiet.	

J.B. Chapman Capt
11 West Yorkshire Regt

WAR DIARY or INTELLIGENCE SUMMARY

Army Form C. 2118

11 W. York Regt Vol 16

Place	Date 1917	Hour	Summary of Events and Information	Remarks and references to Appendices
In the field	Sept 1st		Battalion relieved in YPRES BARRACKS by 8th Bn. K.O.Y.L.I. and proceeded to ST LAWRENCE CAMP. Arrived in Camp 10-11 pm.	
	2nd		In ST LAWRENCE CAMP. General cleaning up. Programme of work commenced. Sports. Working parties	
	3rd		" " Programme of work continued. Sports. Working parties	
	4th		" " ditto	
	5th		" " ditto	
	6th		" " ditto	
	7th		" " ditto	
	8th		" " Battalion Route March. Baths levied. Sports.	
	9th		Battalion relieved 18th D.L.I. in ZILLEBEKE BUND. Hd A & C coys at BUND, B & D Coy in STAFFORD STREET and ½ D. Coy in WINNIPEG ST.	
	10th		General cleaning up. Working parties.	
	11th		" "	
	12th		Cleaning and repairing BUND. Working parties.	
	13th		Battalion relieved 10th W. York Riding Regt in frontline. H.Q. at VALLEY COTTAGES. A, B and D coys in frontline. "C" Coy in Support.	

WAR DIARY or INTELLIGENCE SUMMARY

Army Form C. 2118.

Place	Date 1917	Hour	Summary of Events and Information	Remarks and references to Appendices
St Pierre	Feby 14		In trenches. Artillery active – otherwise quiet.	
	15		" "	
	16		Quiet. 1 Casualty (wounded)	
	17		Relieved by 10th Bn West Riding Regt. HQ "B" & "D" Coys in Bund; "A" Coy ½ "C" Coy in STAFFORD STREET and ½ in MAPLE COPSE. ½ "C" Coy in MAPLE COPSE and ½ in the REDAN	
	18		In Bund. General cleaning up.	
	19		" Cleaning and repairing Bund. Working parties.	
	20		" Bund by division to right. On later orders. 3 of "C" Coy killed.	
	21		Battalion relieved 10th Bn West Riding Regt in line. HQ & Valley Cottages. A, B & C Coys in line. D Coy to Reegan Ravine School for training.	
	22		In trenches. Very quiet. Misty all day.	
	23		" "	
	24		Quiet.	
	25		Relieved by 1st Bn Hampshire Regt (89th Division). Proceeded to ST LAWRENCE CAMP.	
	26		Arrived in Camp at 3.30 am. Cleaning up.	

WAR DIARY
INTELLIGENCE SUMMARY

Army Form C. 2118.

Place	Date	Hour	Summary of Events and Information	Remarks and references to Appendices
	July 28 1917		Battalion left ST LAWRENCE CAMP and marched to HOUTERQUE. Weather had continued hot. Left HOUTERQUE at 9 am and marched to MERCKERGEM. Arrived in Billets at MERCKERGEM at 3.30 pm.	

B. Henry Lut/Col
Comp any
11th Battn Yorks hire Regt

Army Form C. 2118.

WAR DIARY
or
INTELLIGENCE SUMMARY.
(Erase heading not required.)

Instructions regarding War Diaries and Intelligence Summaries are contained in F. S. Regs., Part II. and the Staff Manual respectively. Title pages will be prepared in manuscript.

Place	Date	Hour	Summary of Events and Information	Remarks and references to Appendices
In the Field.	1917 Feby 1st		Battalion relieved in YPRES BARRACKS by 6th Bn. K.O.Y.L.I. and proceeded to ST LAWRENCE CAMP. Arrived in Camp 10 pm.	
	2nd		In ST LAWRENCE CAMP. General cleaning up. Programme of work commenced.	
	3rd		" " Programme of work continued. Sports. Working parties.	
	4th		" " ditto	
	5th		" " ditto	
	6th		" " ditto	
	7th		" " ditto	
	8th		" " Battalion Route March. Battn. Concert. Sports.	
	9th		" Battn. relieved 18th D.L.I. in ZILLEBEKE BUND. H.Q. A + C Coys at BUND. B + D Coy in STAFFORD STREET and to D. Coy in WINNIPEG ST.	
	10th		General cleaning up. Working parties.	
	11th		" "	
	12th		Cleaning and repairing BUND. Working parties.	
	13th		Battalion relieved 10th Bn. West Riding Regt in front line. H.Q. at VALLEY COTTAGES. A. B and D Coys in front line "C" Coy in Support.	

WAR DIARY or INTELLIGENCE SUMMARY.

Army Form C. 2118.

Place	Date	Hour	Summary of Events and Information	Remarks and references to Appendices
In the field	1917 Feby 14		In trenches. Artillery active - otherwise quiet.	
	15		" " "	
	16		" Quiet. 1 Casualty (wounded)	
	17		Relieved by 13th Bn West Riding Regt. H.Q. "B" & "D" Coys in Bund; A. Coy H.Q. & Coy in STAFFORD STREET and ½ in MAPLE COPSE. ½ "C" Coy in MAPLE COPSE ½ in the REDAN	
	18		In Bund. General cleaning up.	
	19		" Cleaning and repairing Bund. Working parties	
	20		" Raid by division on Right. Our lines shelled. 3 of "C" Coy killed.	
	21		Battalion relieved 18th Bn West Riding Regt in line. H.Q. at Valley Cottages, A.B & D Coys in line. D. Coy at Ridges Rendezvous for training.	
	22		In trenches. Very quiet - Mainly all day.	
	23		" " "	
	24		" Quiet.	
	25		Relieved by 1st Bn Hampshire Regt. (3rd Division). Proceed to ST LAWRENCE CAMP	
	26		Arrived in Camp at 3.30 am. Cleaning up.	

WAR DIARY
or
INTELLIGENCE SUMMARY.
(Erase heading not required.)

Army Form C. 2118.

Place	Date	Hour	Summary of Events and Information	Remarks and references to Appendices
In Field	July 1917 27 & 28		Battalion left ST LAWRENCE CAMP and marched to HOUTKERQUE. In billets for night. Continued march. Left HOUTKERQUE at 9 am and marched to MERCKEGHEM. Arrived in Billets at MERCKEGHEM at 3.30 pm.	E. Armytage Capt & Adjt 11th West Yorkshire Regt

Army Form C. 2118.

XI W York Regt
1/11/17

WAR DIARY
or
INTELLIGENCE SUMMARY.
(Erase heading not required.)

Place	Date	Hour	Summary of Events and Information	Remarks and references to Appendices
MERCHERGEM	March			
	1st	—	Battalion left MERCHERGEM and marched to BAVENGHEM.	
BAVENGHEM	2		In Billets at BAVENGHEM. Scheme delivering in. Programme of training commenced. Scheme by G.O.C. by Bde.	
	3		Training programme continued	
	4		Training programme continued — Church Parade.	
	5		Training programme continued — Baths — Sports commenced.	
	6		" "	
	7		" "	
	8		" " Rifle Range attended — Battalion Run —	
	9		Battalion Route March — Football —	
	10		Battalion training as Training Programme —	
	11		Training Programme continued — Battalion Run —	
	12		" "	
	13		" " Church Parade. Battalion Cross Country Run —	
	14		Battalion training on training ground. Musketry on Range — Eng Test. Battalion in attack — Senior Officers Staff Ride with the G.O.C. Senior Division on Range.	

2353 Wt. W2544/1454 700,000 5/15 D. D. & L. A.D.S.S./Forms/C. 2118.

Army Form C. 2118.

WAR DIARY
or
INTELLIGENCE SUMMARY.
(Erase heading not required.)

Place	Date	Hour	Summary of Events and Information	Remarks and references to Appendices
BAYENGHEM	15		Brigade day. Brigade in attack.	
"	16		Battalion programme of training continued. Sports.	
	17		" "	
	18		Church parade. Cleaning up & preparing to move.	
	19		Battalion left BAYENGHEM and marched to MERCKEGHEM - rte - WATTEN - HOECK - MERCKEGHEM.	
MERCKEGHEM	20		Battalion left MERCKEGHEM and marched to HERZEELE - rte - BOLLEZEELE - ZEGGARS CAPPEL - ESQUELBECQ - HERZEELE	
HERZEELE	21		Battalion left HERZEELE and marched to "Y" Camp - rte - HOUTERQUE - WATOU - ST JAN Gr BIEREN - "Y" Camp	
"Y" Camp	22		General Cleaning up. Training continued. Sports	
	23		Training continued - Staff plans for Offrs & Brigade under C.O.	
	24		" Sports	
	25		Church Parade - Gas Shell Drill - Lewis Gun instruction for Officers & NCOs under Sgt Instructor WILLIS - (Machine Gun School)	
	26		Training continues - Sports	

Army Form C. 2118.

WAR DIARY
or
INTELLIGENCE SUMMARY.
(Erase heading not required.)

Place	Date	Hour	Summary of Events and Information	Remarks and references to Appendices
Y Camp	27		Training Continued – Baths – Staff Ride under Capt Mindoff. 8th York's Emperor	
	28		Entire Patrol scheme for Signallers. Sports	
	29		Inspection by G.O.C. 2nd Army – Bivouac Training Continued. Sports	
	30		" Working Parties. Sports	
	31		" Baths – Sports.	

W.T Sanselm
[signature]
[signature]
Lt Col. 1st Amherst Yorkshire Regt

WAR DIARY
or
INTELLIGENCE SUMMARY
(Erase heading not required.)

Army Form C. 2118.

XI W Y[or]R Reg[t]

Place	Date	Hour	Summary of Events and Information	Remarks and references to Appendices
"Y" Camp nr Poperinghe	April 1st/15	5"	The Battalion was in training at "Y" Camp (near Poperinghe) during the previous period of the day. In the afternoon the OC (Capt. Infantry) marched in to the Battalion the following officers who had just been sent by the Unit, and so any the first draft of the 2nd Reserve Supplement (officers) who joined the Battalion pending the arrival of supplies daily.	
Ottawa Camp Nr Poperinghe	6th 7.10 PB		(Open training) Church service in morning. The Battalion left "Y" Camp & marched to OTTAWA Camp in the afternoon — Battalion at OTTAWA Camp. Training was however held during stay at OTTAWA. Battalion furnished working supplies. Battery 15" working parties, Battalion working with 11th Sherwood Foresters in the line.	
Hill 60. Ypres Salient.	15 9/B.88 pm		Centre Battalion of the whole 60 Sector Battalion in the line during the 8 days tour and the total 1 man killed and 5 men wounded. Anything further	

WAR DIARY or INTELLIGENCE SUMMARY.

Army Form C. 2118.

Place	Date	Hour	Summary of Events and Information	Remarks and references to Appendices
"Y" Camp nr Poperinghe	April 1st to 5th		The Battalion was in training at "Y" Camp (near Poperinghe) during first five days of April. On the 3rd day the G.O.C. Infantry Brigade visited the Battalion. The Interbrigade Shield which has been won by the Unit, and 1st and 2nd army, the first year of the Divisional Championship (Football) was played. The Battalion received the R.F.A. weekly trophies were supplied daily.	
	6th		(Some training.) Church service in morning. The Battalion left Y Camp & marched to OTTAWA Camp in the afternoon.	
OTTAWA CAMP Nr POPERINGHE	7th to 13th		Battalion at OTTAWA Camp. Training was however well during stay at OTTAWA. Battalion received Baths on "D" working parties were supplied daily.	
	14th		Battalion relieved 11th Bn. SHERWOOD FORESTERS in the line between the Caterpillar Railway & the Ypres-Comines Canal 60 Sector.	
HILL 60 YPRES SALIENT	15th 6.00pm		Battalion in the line during the 8 days tour we had 1 man killed and 5 wounded. Weather for most of

The line with occasional raids, but activity was shown by enemy snipers - the chances on No Man's Killed - killed. Training matters have again after were delivered nightly. Construction was fairly heavy bringing reopening of trenches which were partly damaged by enemy and forming parapets to not entomb the dead.
The below to mine crater 19 the enemy = blew own

23
Up to —

24" Battalion relieved in line by 11" SHERWOOD FORESTERS, and proceeded to ST LAWRENCE (G.11.c centre mat SHM BELGIUM) arriving at Camp at about 5 A.M. Vehicles and

25"to 28" Battalion at ST LAWRENCE CAMP. Guns cleaning up. Programme of training carried on daily.

29. Battalion left ST LAWRENCE CAMP and marched to STEENVOORDE.

30. Battalion at STEENVOORDE - Guns cleaning up - training carried on.

W. Clarkson
Lt Col
OC 11th Bn Worcester Rgt

Army Form C. 2118.

WAR DIARY
or
INTELLIGENCE SUMMARY.
(Erase heading not required.)

Place	Date	Hour	Summary of Events and Information	Remarks and references to Appendices
	23rd		the line will account lost. Much activity was shown by enemy snipers - who claimed our two killed - whilst the enemy machine gun fire after we relieved night. Construction was faulty not being repaired of trenches which were hastily undergone and furnace furnaces to not entering the time. The fellow a mine crater 19th the enemy on blew over	
	24th		the 10th Battalion relieved in time by 11th SHERWOOD FORESTERS, and proceeded to ST LAWRENCE (G.11.c entire map SF N.W. BELGIUM) arriving at Camp about 5 AM the 25th inst.	
	25/6/28		Battalion ST LAWRENCE CAMP Enemy cleaning up. Programme of training carried on daily.	
	29th		Battalion left ST LAWRENCE CAMP and marched to STEENVOORDE.	
	30		Battalion at STEENVOORDE - Enemy cleaning up - training commenced	

W. Sainsbury
Lt Col 11th Sherwood Foresters

11 N York Regt
Vol 19

WAR DIARY
or
INTELLIGENCE SUMMARY.
(Erase heading not required.)

Place	Date 1917	Hour	Summary of Events and Information	Remarks and references to Appendices
STEENVOORDE	May 1st to 5th		Battalion in training at STEENVOORDE. The Battalion was inspected by G.O.C. 23rd Division. Route marches were made daily.	
	6"		Battalion (less 2 coys) moved from STEENVOORDE and marched to DEVONSHIRE CAMP. C & D coys remained in STEENVOORDE.	
	7"		C & D coys leave STEENVOORDE and are attached to a unit further to the rear. Heavy shelling for that. Unknown of fatalities. Commence to convey working parties with Australians consisting large Sessions horking.	
	8 to 15"		This period is taken up by working parties commencing on 7" and ending 15" and the battalion suffered 13 casualties & 03 being killed & rest wounded.	
	16"		Battalion (less 2 Companies) marched to ONTARIO CAMP.	
	16" & 17"		Battalion (less 2 Coys) at ONTARIO Camp. Time devoted to cleaning up. Company Drill	
	18"		Battalion (less 2 Coys) relieved 13th Bn. Reserve position H.Q. w/ B and D Coys at RAILWAY DUGOUTS.	

Army Form C. 2118.

WAR DIARY
or
INTELLIGENCE SUMMARY.
(Erase heading not required.)

Instructions regarding War Diaries and Intelligence Summaries are contained in F. S. Regs., Part II and the Staff Manual respectively. Title pages will be prepared in manuscript.

Place	Date	Hour	Summary of Events and Information	Remarks and references to Appendices
ZILLEBEKE BUND	19	6.75"	Battalion (less 2 Coys) to Reserve positions. Some demolition & working parties. Event.... artillery otherwise uneventful. Some infantry observed.	
	21		Battalion relieved in Reserve position by 5th K.O.Y.L.I.	
	25		Battalion moved at 2 am from Reserve position and proceeded by train to BOESINGHE arr. at K.35 c.3.6	
BOESINGHE	26. 27.	6.31"	On 27th Coy to Coys reformed and spent these days Battalion received special training and trenches in training area. The 29th was teny rendered to a Brigade Day.	

2353. Wt. W2544/1454. 700,000. 5/15. D.D. & L. A.D.S.S./Forms/C. 2118.

Lt Col Gallaher Events for Capt.
for 11th King's Own Yorks L.I.

Army Form C. 2118.

WAR DIARY
or
INTELLIGENCE SUMMARY.
(Erase heading not required.)

Instructions regarding War Diaries and Intelligence Summaries are contained in F. S. Regs., Part II. and the Staff Manual respectively. Title pages will be prepared in manuscript.

Place	Date	Hour	Summary of Events and Information	Remarks and references to Appendices
STEENVOORDE	May 5th		Battalion in training at STEENVOORDE from 1st to 5th inst, on 5th inst the Battalion was inspected by Genl. D'Oyer Snow — Route marches were made daily.	
	6		Battalion (less D Coy) moved from STEENVOORDE and marched to DEVONSHIRE CAMP.	
	7th		C & D Coys Remained at h STEENVOORDE bill ? C & D Coys Left STEENVOORDE and were attached to entrenching Coys — Heavy artillery on duty. Remainder of Battalion commenced on daily working parties.	
	8th to 9th		The permit to [be] taken up by working parties commenced on 7th inst., on the 9th the Battalion suffered 13 casualties, 2 O.R.s being killed & 11 O.R.s wounded.	
	15		Battalion (less C Coy) marched to ONTARIO Camp.	
	16th 17th		Battalion (less D Coy) at ONTARIO Camp. Time devoted to cleaning up & Company Drill.	
ZILLEBEKE BUND	18		Battalion (less D Coy) relieved D.L.I. in Reserve position. H.Q. W Bund.	
	19th & 20th		2nd & Corps of RAILWAY DUGOUTS. Battalion (less D Coy) in Reserve positions. Time devoted to working parties. Enemy artillery active. Otherwise nothing of importance occurred.	

Army Form C. 2118.

WAR DIARY
or
INTELLIGENCE SUMMARY.
(Erase heading not required.)

Instructions regarding War Diaries and Intelligence Summaries are contained in F.S. Regs., Part II. and the Staff Manual respectively. Title pages will be prepared in manuscript.

Place	Date	Hour	Summary of Events and Information	Remarks and references to Appendices
DUESECK, BUND	24		Battalion relieved in Reserve Junction by 8th KOYLI.	
	25		Battalion moved 3 am from Reserve Railway approaching train to BOESCOEPE from H.Q. at R 35 + 36.	
	26th & 27th		Bn Sgt C.O. Coy reported and during these days Battalion general special training over Green haased trenches in training area. The Sgt went two days to Bn Brigade Army	

A.H.G. Walker Lieut Colonel
for " on transportation "

69/23

Head Quarters,
69th Infantry Brigade.
July 6th, 1917.

Head Quarters, "A"
23rd Division.

      Herewith War Diary of 11th West Yorkshire Regiment.

                                              Capt.,
                                  Brigade Major, for
                        G.O.C.69th Infantry Brigade.

Army Form C. 2118.

XI W. York Rg.

Vol 20

WAR DIARY
or
INTELLIGENCE SUMMARY.
(Erase heading not required.)

Place	Date	Hour	Summary of Events and Information	Remarks and references to Appendices
Boeschepe	June 1st		Battalion left Boeschepe area and marched to Camp about L.33.d.1.9.	
L.27.d.1.9.	2		In Camp. Cleaning up Company parades Battalion Drill.	
L. Camp.	3.		Moved to "L" Camp.	
Zillebeke Bund	4th		Battalion moved in to ZILLEBEKE BUND	
Aussie	5th		On the night of the 5/6th the Battalion left ZILLEBEKE BUND and took up its position in the ditch allotted to it for the attack.	
	6th		The 6th was spent in making final preparations and passed quietly and with few casualties.	
	7th		On the night of the 6th/7th the Battalion moved into its assembly position and at 2.30 am on the 7th was ready for the attack. Not a single casualty occurred during the whole of this night prior to Zero hour. At 3.10 am (7th Pats) simultaneously with the explosion of the mines at Hill 60 and the CATERPILLAR the attack was launched entirely according to plan. By 4.30 am it was reported that the whole of the Red, or 1st Objective had been taken, and by 5 am. the three Companies (A.B & C.) in the front line, were	

WAR DIARY
or
INTELLIGENCE SUMMARY

Army Form C. 2118.

Place	Date	Hour	Summary of Events and Information	Remarks and references to Appendices
	7.		consolidating the blue line. By 7 am the 12" D.L.I. had passed through my Blue line towards the Black line. Up to noon casualties though very heavy were not opposed otherwise remained at the same figure for the rest of the 7".	
	8/9.		From the 8" onwards heavy shell fire was brought to bear on us by enemy artillery on the left flank, and casualties were very heavy, particularly in respect of 6"/9" when a counter attack threatened & hostile fire increased greatly in intensity.	
	9/10.		On the night of the 9"/10" the Battalion less D. Coy was relieved by 13" D.L.I. and was withdrawn to Bulaeon Farm. "D" Coy was relieved by 11" Northumberland Fusiliers on 10"/11".	
	11/12		Here Battalion remained until night of 12/13 when parts of the 7" Brigade of the "Div" took its place, and the Battn left the line for "P" Camp, in the neighbourhood of OUDERDOM. This concludes the action of HILL 60 so far as concerns this Battalion.	
			Casualties for the whole of the action 6"/13" June 1917	
			OFFICERS.	O.R.
			6 killed, 1 wounded & Missing, believed killed, 9 wounded.	30 killed, 193 wounded, 10 missing, 17 died of wounds. Total 253 Casualties.

Army Form C. 2118.

WAR DIARY
or
INTELLIGENCE SUMMARY.
(Erase heading not required.)

Instructions regarding War Diaries and Intelligence Summaries are contained in F.S. Regs., Part II. and the Staff Manual respectively. Title pages will be prepared in manuscript.

Place	Date	Hour	Summary of Events and Information	Remarks and references to Appendices
METEREN AREA	June 13		Battalion moved from R. Camp to METEREN AREA. H.Q. at X.2.C.2.2. Sheet 27.	
	14,15,16		General Recreational training	
	17		Church parades.	
	18,19,20,23		Training, musketry Range. Recreational training	
	24		Church Parades.	
	25		General Recreations training. Divisional Horse Show.	
	26,27,28		General Recreational training. Baths.	
ONTARIO Camp.	29		Battalion moved to ONTARIO Camp.	
BATTLE WOOD Sub. Distr.	30		Battalion moved in to line. Relieved 1st Bn. North Staffordshire Regt. in BATTLE WOOD subsector. "A" + "B" Coys in front line. "C" Support. "D" Reserve. H.Q. in IMPERIAL TRENCH. The casualties whilst relieving. In trench. Enemy artillery + aircraft active. Trenches in poor condition. Work on deepening + improving trench commenced.	

[signatures]

WAR DIARY
or
INTELLIGENCE SUMMARY.
(Erase heading not required.)

XI W York Rgt
Army Form C. 2118.

Place	Date	Hour	Summary of Events and Information	Remarks and references to Appendices
BATTLE WOOD SUB SECTOR OF LINE	July 1st		Battn in BATTLE WOOD subsector of line. A&B Coys in front line, C Coy in support. D Coy in Reserve. H.Q. at IMPERIAL TRENCH. Artillery very active.	
	2nd		In trenches. Artillery & enemy trench aircraft very active. Drafts of officers joined Battalion as reinforcements.	
	3rd		Battalion relieved in line by 20th London Regt and proceeded on relief to MICMAC CAMP arriving in Camp on morning of 4th. 2 ORs Casualties for tour of 4 days. 2 ORs killed + 3 ORs wounded. Draft of 187 ORs	
	4th		Battalion moved by train & march route to STEENVOORDE area. joined Bde.	
	5th & 6th		Battalion in training in STEENVOORDE area	
	6th		Inspection of medal ribbons and inspection of Draft by G.O.C. Division.	
	7th		Company parades route marches. Draft of 61 ORs joined. S.M. intensely of Army Gymnastic Staff arrived in Rear for 6 little courses in P.T.	
	8th		School parades	
	9th		Company parades battalion Drill. Visit of G.O.C. to Div. to present. Meeting Cross & D. C's ribbons	

WAR DIARY
or
INTELLIGENCE SUMMARY

Army Form C. 2118.

Place	Date	Hour	Summary of Events and Information	Remarks and references to Appendices
	July			
	10, 11.		Company parades. Battalion Drill. Recreation training.	
	12		Battalion left STEENVOORDE and moved by train from GODEWAERSVELDE to Anderson Siding, thence to MICMAC CAMP. Arrived in Camp 7.20pm	
	13		B. + C. Coys proceed to trenches. 1 Platoon to Brigade Band School	
	14		A Coy moved to DICKEBUSCH for working parties. H.Q. move to LARCH WOOD	
	15		C Coy move from MICMAC to LARCH WOOD. Both supplied working parties.	
	16		Battalion relieves the 8th Yorks & Lancs in line. C + D Coys in front line, A Coy Support. A Coy Reserve. H.Q. at MOVABLE SUPPORT.	
			Battalion in the line. Heavy artillery duels. 15 casualties. 10th prs killed.	
	19.		Battn relieved in front line positions by 8th Yorks & Lancs. Moved to support positions. HQ + D at TORR TOP tunnels, A at RUDKIN HOUSE, B at METROPOLITAN LEFT + C at CANADA ST.	
			Battn in support working parties.	
	20, 21			
	22		Battn relieved by 8th Buffs (R.W. KENT) Regt. and proceeded to MICMAC Camp. Total Casualties for line 16 killed 51 wounded
	23		Battn arrived in Camp at 3am. Batn proceeded by Route march to BERTHEN area. H.Q. at X.2.C.O.4.	

2353 Wt.W2544/1454 700,000 5/15 D.D.&L. A.D.S.S./Forms/C.2118.

Army Form C. 2118.

WAR DIARY
or
INTELLIGENCE SUMMARY.
(Erase heading not required.)

Instructions regarding War Diaries and Intelligence Summaries are contained in F. S. Regs., Part II. and the Staff Manual respectively. Title pages will be prepared in manuscript.

Place	Date	Hour	Summary of Events and Information	Remarks and references to Appendices
	July			
	24		Cleaning of Company made. Baths.	
	25		Inspection by C.O.C Division. Presence spoilt by heavy rain. Inspection made by Companies at Coy Billets.	
	26		Baths. moved to BOIS DINGHEM area.	
	27		A & C Coys firing on Range. B & D Coys training. Arrived in billets at 7.30 pm. Report typing on B.F. Course	
	28		Remainder training in training area.	
	29		Church parade. C & D Coys on Range.	
	30		Company training. A & B Coys patrol scheme under Commanding Officer.	
	31		Battalion on Range. Firing Musketry & Visual Training.	

Army Form C. 2118.

WAR DIARY
or
INTELLIGENCE SUMMARY.
(Erase heading not required.)

Instructions regarding War Diaries and Intelligence Summaries are contained in F.S. Regs., Part II and the Staff Manual respectively. Title pages will be prepared in manuscript.

XI W York 21

Place	Date	Hour	Summary of Events and Information	Remarks and references to Appendices
	Aug 4th		Batn. at BOISDINGHEM area.	
	5th		Company Parades in vicinity of billets.	
	6th		Field Day. Battalion practises the attack.	
	7th		Inspection by G.O.C. 2nd Army.	
	8th		Coy Parades & Baths at HOULLE.	
	9th		Moved to billets at HOULLE in the EPERLECQUES area. Arrived in heavy rain at 4.5pm. Evening spent cleaning up and drying clothes.	
	10th		Company Parades. Lecture on the M.H. by DAMS. 23rd Divn for Officers.	
	11th		Church Parade. G.O.C. 69th Bgde presented medal ribbons to Officers & men.	
	12th		Company Parade - Intensive Digging - Range at P10. Lecture by Corps Gas Officer for Senior Officers.	
	13th		Battalion Field Day. Practising the deployment into Artillery formation from the rear of march. Stores Visit dumped. "B" & "D" Coys training in training area	
	14th		"C" Coy on Range at K.36.	
	15th		"A" Coy proceed to 18th Corps School for demonstration purposes.	

2353. Wt. W2544/1454 700,000 5/15 D.D.&L. A.D.S.S./Forms/C. 2118.

Army Form C. 2118.

WAR DIARY
or
INTELLIGENCE SUMMARY
(Erase heading not required.)

Instructions regarding War Diaries and Intelligence Summaries are contained in F. S. Regs., Part II and the Staff Manual respectively. Title pages will be prepared in manuscript.

Place	Date	Hour	Summary of Events and Information	Remarks and references to Appendices
	Aug. 6th		Baths at Houlle. "B" Range at P.12.b allotted to Lewis Guns. "B" & "D" Coys in training area practising the attack.	
	17th		Battalion Parade. Packs deployment into Artillery formation. The maintenance of direction. 8.30pm Packs forming up on tapes in training area. Range. Q.O. allotted to bat. Slots.	
	18th		"C" & "D" Companies practising Artillery formation. "B" Company advance digging.	
	19th		Brigade Field Day.	
	20th		Company parades in the morning. 7.30pm Brigade Exercise forming up on tapes.	
	21st		Brigade Field Day.	
	22nd		Company Parades and firing on the Ranges.	
	23rd			
	24th		Battn. moved from Houlle. Proceeded by March route to water station. Entrained about 11 p.m. to Steele. Marched the Battalion detrained and marched to billets at Wippenhoek Area.	
	25th		Battn. moved again from there rifles to camps in Dickebush Area. Proceeded by	

2353 Wt. W2544/1454 700,000 5/15 D. D. & L. A.D.S.S./Forms/C. 2118.

Army Form C. 2118.

WAR DIARY
or
INTELLIGENCE SUMMARY.
(Erase heading not required.)

Instructions regarding War Diaries and Intelligence Summaries are contained in F. S. Regs., Part II. and the Staff Manual respectively. Title pages will be prepared in manuscript.

Place	Date	Hour	Summary of Events and Information	Remarks and references to Appendices
	Aug. 25th		Motor Lorries which were waiting on the Abeele - Poperinghe Road - and the whole Battalion was conveyed in these to the Camp.	
	" 26th		Cleaning up and awaiting further orders to move. Officers N.C.O.s visited Battle model Corps.	
	" 27th		Battalion (less transport & stores) moved to CHATEAU SEGARD area. Here it was accommodated in dugouts etc.	
	28th to 3rd		Awaiting further orders to move further up the line at any moment. Company training in the mornings, and parties visited the II Corps Battle model	

W.T. Marsh
Lieut. & Adjutant,
12th (Service) Bn. West Yorkshire Regt.

for O.C. 12th (Service) Bn. West Yorkshire Regt.

War Diary

~~Congratulatory~~

~~Messages.~~

11th Batt West
Yorks Regt
September 1917

WAR DIARY or INTELLIGENCE SUMMARY

Army Form C. 2118.

69/23
XI W Font By
Vol 23

Place	Date Sept	Hour	Summary of Events and Information	Remarks and references to Appendices
CHATEAU SEGARD	1st		Battalion in reserve at Chateau Segard - Dickebush Area	
STEENVOORDE	2nd		Battalion moved by March Route to Steenvoorde Area	
LEDERZEELE	3rd		Battalion marched to Lederzeele Area	
"	4-10		Battalion in Lederzeele Area training under Company and Battalion arrangements in preparation for pending Autumn Range work. On 10th, Battalion took part in a practice attack over model trenches. Parties of 10 walked from line each day to view the ground over which the next attack is to be delivered. Demonstration on Shell fire by Durands the officer on Anti aircraft sights and the Lewis gun - Sparks -	
"	11-12		Brigade in the attack over 18th Corps Model Trenches	
"	13		Battalion moved from Lederzeele to Steenvoorde (West) area by work route.	
STEENVOORDE	14		Battalion moved from Steenvoorde (west) to Ontario Camp (Reninghelst)	
ONTARIO CAMP	15		Battalion practice going over ground at dawn. Visit by Companies to Model Trenches. Gas helmet Inspection.	
MICMAC CAMP	16		Battalion marched from Ontario Camp to Nr. Micmac Area arriving at 10 am. Church parades.	

Army Form C. 2118.

WAR DIARY
or
INTELLIGENCE SUMMARY.
(Erase heading not required.)

Place	Date	Hour	Summary of Events and Information	Remarks and references to Appendices
MICMAC CAMP	17		Battalion at MICMAC CAMP. Company parades ready at Battletrack.	
	18/9/17		The Battalion in accordance with 69 Brigade Instructions left MICMAC Camp at 9 am and proceeded to relieve the 8th Yorks, then holding the line INVERNESS COPSE Sector, completing the relief during the afternoon. The Battalion strength on going into action was 31 Officers and 590 O.Rs. The Battalion suffered 35 casualties before relief was completed.	
			2. The 19th was spent in making final arrangements for the assembly and attack, and passed without incident until 10 pm when heavy rain fell for about an hour whilst the troops were forming up for the assault. After making all Companies to Companies Lt Col M.H. Barker D.S.O handed over the Command to Major H.A. Mundor M.C. and was withdrawn to Brigade H.Q where he awaited the E.O.C. until the conclusion of the operations on 20th.	
			3. The assembly of the assaulting troops was completed without loss but the Enemy opened a tentative barrage about 4 am 20th and on the Western Edge of INVERNESS COPSE which lasted for about 30 minutes and caused somewhat heavy losses, nearly 50 O.Rs being killed + wounded.	

WAR DIARY or INTELLIGENCE SUMMARY

Army Form C. 2118.

Place	Date	Hour	Summary of Events and Information	Remarks and references to Appendices
	18/9/18		Fortunately the enemy ceased shelling at 4.30 a.m. and the last hour before ZERO was passed in quietness. 4. At 5.40 a.m. (ZERO hour) on the 20th Sept. our barrage opened and Zero + 3' our troops advanced. The bopse was very strongly held but the enemy appeared demoralised and very ready to surrender. The attack progressed absolutely according to plan on both flanks but a slight gap was left between the left and centre Company which was at once filled by first lining with two platoons of the Reserve Company. The RED LINE was captured and consolidation began by 6.10 a.m. and patrols were thrown forward all along the line. A bombing up party to the standing barrage, a task which was most successfully accomplished, many dug-outs being cleared and prisoners taken. During this time the 9th Yorkshire Regiment were closing up and preparing to advance. The next objective (BLUE LINE) however the barrage lifted at ZERO + 90' the attack on this line was begun and the "RED LINE" was passed. 5. The Battalion remained in the line clearing the Battlefield until the 21st/25 when it was relieved by units of the 9th & 100th Brigade (33rd Div.)	

WAR DIARY or INTELLIGENCE SUMMARY

Army Form C. 2118.

Place	Date	Hour	Summary of Events and Information	Remarks and references to Appendices
	16/24	6.	Officers present in the action were:— Lt Col M. W. Barker D.S.O. Commanding. Major H. H. Hudson M.C. 2nd in Command. Lieut. b. Y. Lunsbury. Adjutant. 2/Lt. V. Hope-Stephen. Intelligence Officer. **A Coy** Capt. Ca Thron M.C. (Killed) Lt. W. Barraclough (wounded) 2/Lt. J. Case (Died of wounds) 2nd Lt. L. Calvert **B Coy** Capt. Balancino M.C. 2nd Lt. Jo. Irving (wounded (remained at duty) 2nd Lt. E. J. McCrae 2/Lt. B. Riddel (Bengthurst) Medical Officer Capt. D.O. Riddel D.S.O. wounded 5th relieved by Capt. Cameron 9th Field Ambulance. **C Coy** Lt. Omgli 2/Lt. R. Kilbery 2nd Lt. J. Thomas (Killed) 2/Lt. B. Hamilton **D Coy** Capt. Ch Armstrong M.C. (Evacuated remained at duty) Capt. Kirkmun 2/Lt. J.f. Donne 2/Lt. C.J. Hoggan Casualties 19/24th were as follows:— Officers 2 Killed 3 Died of wounds 1 wounded 2 wounded & remained at duty ___ 7 O.Ro. Killed 56. Killed 4 Died of wounds. 308 wounded 10 missing 3 wounded & remained at duty ___ 381	

Army Form C. 2118.

WAR DIARY
or
INTELLIGENCE SUMMARY.
(Erase heading not required.)

Instructions regarding War Diaries and Intelligence Summaries are contained in F. S. Regs., Part II. and the Staff Manual respectively. Title pages will be prepared in manuscript.

Place	Date	Hour	Summary of Events and Information	Remarks and references to Appendices
MICMAC CAMP	25		Battalion at Micmac Camp. Baths at Dickebusch. During day moved by Michroute to Ontario Camp. Draft of 105 O.R. "Untrained" joined Battalion.	
	26		Battalion cleaning up & reorganising.	
	27		At 9 am Battalion moved to SCOTTISH WOOD where dinners were taken, thence to take over the line in support, from mixed element of 33rd Division in the INVERNESS COPSE Sector. "D" Coy on left. "C" on right. "A" behind "D", and "B" behind "C". The casualties going in — total strength going into line Officers 19, O.R.s 469. Work of salvage and cleaning battlefield continued. Preparation for 5th Division attack begun.	
	28		During night of 28/29. "A" Coy relieved "D" Coy and "D" Coy moved forward 500 yards. During the night the enemy bombarded very heavy with gas shells.	
	29		Work continued as on 28th. 17 O.R. "B" Coy gassed and sent out of line. "A" Coy lost 6 Killed and 5 wounded.	
	30		Uneventful day. Visited by Co. of 13th Cluster, relieving Unit of 5th Division.	

W.T. Samson
for O.C. 11th Aust Bn A & A Kind of

ORDERS FOR THE ATTACK
ISSUED BY

LIEUT. COL. M.G.H. BARKER. D.S.O.

COMMANDING

11th Bn WEST YORKSHIRE REGIMENT.

SECRET   OPERATION ORDER NO 1   COPY NO. 5
BY
MAJOR. H.H. HUDSON. M.C
COMMANDING 11th BN WEST YORKSHIRE REGT

MAP REFERENCE SHEET

1. The Battalion will take part in the attack to be delivered by 69th Inf Brigade at a date to be notified later.

2. The Battalion will attack and capture the RED LINE from FITZCLARENCE FARM exclusive to HERENTHAGE CHATEAU inclusive.

3. ASSEMBLY.

Exact assembly positions will be notified later. Companies will assemble either on tapes or in trenches, yet to be dug, approximately on the alignment shown in attached map "A"

"C" Coy between JASPER LANE and JAP AVENUE.
"A" Coy between JASPER LANE and JASPER AVENUE.
"D" Coy across JASPER AVENUE and to right of it.
"B" Coy in continuation of New Trench between JAP AVENUE and JASPER LANE.

4. OBJECTIVES.

Each assaulting Company is allotted a definite area to attack, clear and consolidate.

Boundaries are as shown in Map. A.

"C" Company on left will consolidate the RED LINE, having as its special objectives

(a) Group of dugouts about J.14.d.55.55.
(b) Group of dugouts near S.A.A. dump.

Both these positions will be converted into Strong Points.

(c) The formation of a Strong Point on RED LINE in close proximity to FITZCLARENCE FARM.

A. Company in centre will make Strong Points at
(d) CENTRAL CHATEAU.
(e) J.14.d.55.35.
(f) By MENIN ROAD near S.A.A. dump.

? Telephone box also as an objective.

"D" Company on right will make Strong Points at
    (g) GREEN MOUND
    (h) HERENTHAGE CHATEAU
    (j) AID POST.

? 4th platoon. which to be ?

"B" Company in reserve will take over from mopping up parties of assaulting troops and consolidate
    (k) J. 14. c. 45. 55.
    (l) J. 14. c. 66. 60.
    (m) J. 14. c. 65. 90.

"B" Company will form a mobile reserve force which must be prepared to take immediate action on its own initiative in case of counter-attack.

Every unit must have a definite objective allotted to it. Each man must know exactly where to go, and what to do when he gets there.

Each Company must ensure that the whole of its area is thoroughly mopped up, sufficient troops being detailed to this end.

5. Special points requiring attention.

To be a separate ? objective.

    (1) Group of dugouts behind TELEPHONE EXCHANGE.
    (2) Ridge running North and South through TANK TRAP.

These will be cleared and only converted into Strong Points if the ground is suitable.

(2) will probably form a useful Lewis Gun position from which the Reserve Company can cover RED LINE.

6. FLANKS.

    LEFT O.C. "C" Company will detail 1 Officer and a special party to obtain touch with 1st AUSTRALIAN DIVISION, attacking on left, at FITZCLARENCE FARM

    RIGHT O.C. "D" Company will detail 1 Officer and a special party to obtain touch with 10th NORTHUMBERLAND FUSILIERS, attacking on right, at HERENTHAGE CHATEAU.

INTER COMPANY

O.C. Companies will be responsible that their flanks are linked up and covered with Lewis Guns.

7. CONSOLIDATION

During the consolidation of RED LINE Lewis Guns and sniping groups must be pushed at least 100 yards forward to cover this work.

Troops not engaged in consolidation or other work must be nursed in dugouts in order to ensure that a body of fresh troops is in hand to beat off any counter-attack.

8. FORMATION

"C", "A" and "D" Companies will assault in two waves.

"B" Company will follow "C" Company in one wave.

9. STOKES MORTARS.

[margin note: 2 on 66-61 / 2 on H.C. / ?]

Four guns of 70th T.M.B. will be placed at disposal of O.C. 11th WEST YORKSHIRE REGT near JASPER LANE at J.14.c.10.60 to maintain a rapid barrage on the enemy dugout at J.14.c.55.90 and on trench 66-61 from ZERO to ZERO + 4.

Two guns of the 69th T.M.B. will advance as soon as possible to vicinity of TANK TRAP and will be at disposal of O.C. 11th WEST YORKSHIRE REGT.

(One) ? ~~Two~~ guns will advance to RED LINE just ~~south~~ of CENTRAL CHATEAU, after its capture, and will be at disposal of O.C. 9th YORKSHIRE REGIMENT.

10. MACHINE GUNS

Two Vickers Guns will occupy each of the following Strong Points after their capture.
  HERENTHAGE CHATEAU
  CENTRAL CHATEAU
  AID POST

11. HEADQUARTERS.
Headquarters will be at J.13.d.7.7.
A Forward Post will be established at J.14.c.4.5. as Report Centre to which a telephone line will be maintained.

Lieut & Adjt
11th Bn West Yorkshire Regt.

Issued. Sept 18th 1917
Copies to:-
No 1 O.C. "A" Coy.   No 6. Major H H Sudson M.C
   2 O.C. "B" Coy   7. Adjutant.
   3 O.C. "C" Coy   8. War Diary
   4 O.C. "D" Coy   9. File.
   5 Commanding Officer

1 N.C.O. + 1 man per batt. intelligence particularly to look for papers. & send to Brigade HQ direct -

1½' Very Lights.
S.O.S. used from it.
patrols. — with definite objectives.

1 lorry per battln for those unable to march

Co. again to get in touch with Co. of Australians & 10th N.F's then going into action & J 20 b. 16. 80. (hq Brigade orders)

Tetroh- me Aid Post in H.Q but in consolidate & hold it.

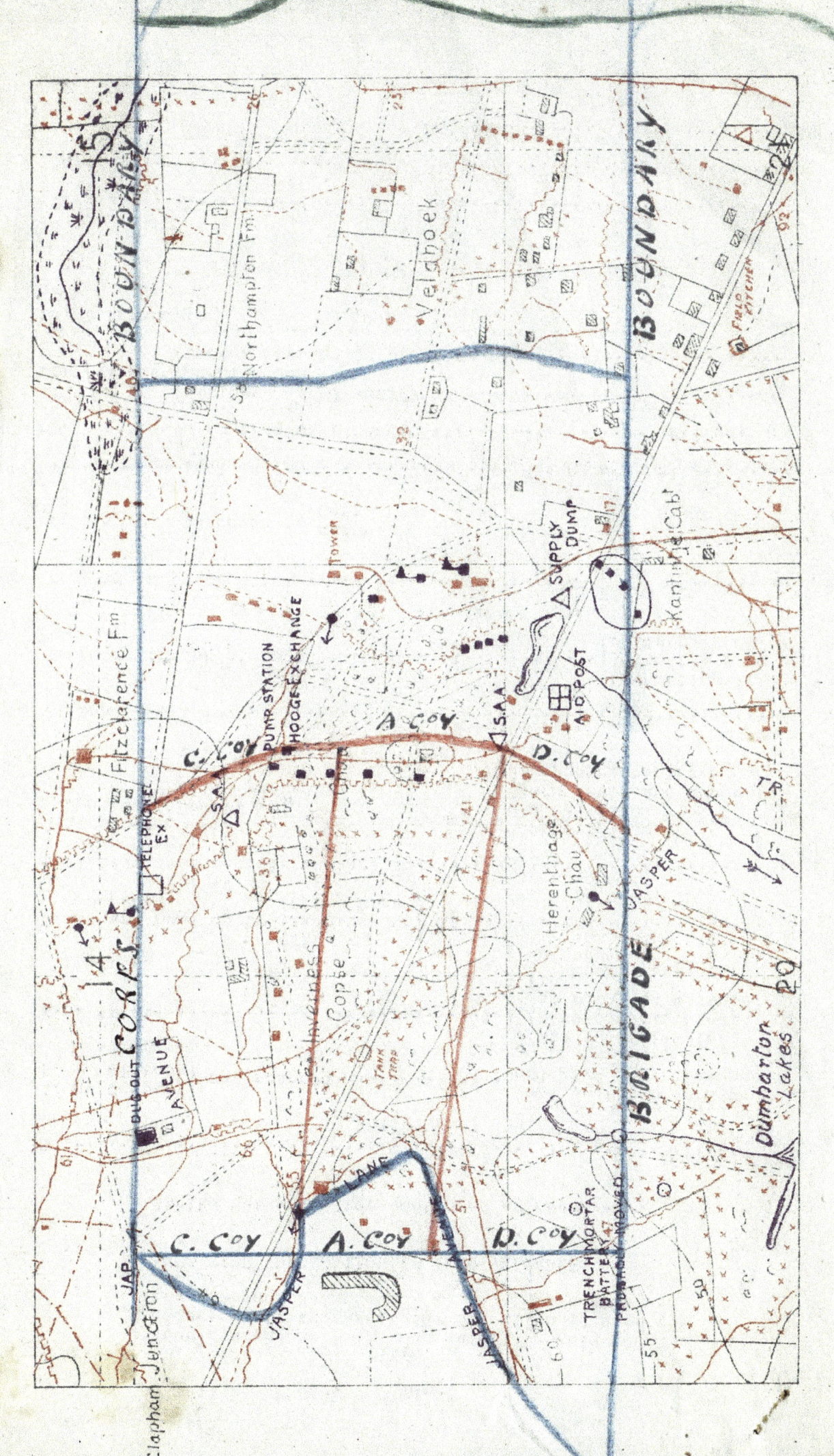

MESSAGE FORM.

Your Message must be such as will enable the Addressee to know what the Situation is with You and your Neighbours.

NEGATIVE INFORMATION IS ALSO VALUABLE.

Strike out and alter sentences as necessary.

TO :-..

1. My Company) has reached............... Mark position on Map
   Platoon)   and give Map reference.

2. I am at.............................and (and consolidating,
                                           (have consolidated,
                                           (am ready to advance
                                           (to

3. We are held up by (Wire   ) at........................
                     (Machine Gun)
                     (Rifle Fire)

4. I have sent patrols forward to.............................

5. I need:- S.A.A.   Stokes shells.
            Bombs.   Stakes, wire.
            Rifle grenades.   Spare Lewis gun drums.
            Water.   Stretcher bearers.
            Very lights, S.O.S. signals, rockets.

   Send above to..

6. Enemy troops strength estimated at........... (assembling at
                                                 (advancing from
                                                 (retiring from

7. I am in touch with.....................on Right at.........
                                             Left

8. I am not in touch on Right.
                       Left.

9. Am being shelled from................ Nature of shell..........

10. I estimate my present strength at...................rifles.

11. Hostile (Battery   ) active at ....and
            (Machine Gun)
            (Trench Mortar) is shooting at........................

12. I intend to

TIME........... a.m. (p.m.)   Name..........................
Date..................   Platoon........ Company.........
                                Battalion......................

SECRET   ADDITIONS TO OPERATION ORDER No.1.   Copy No 10

1. DRESS. Fighting Order. Only essentials will
be carried in the haversack.
Before leaving CAMP each man will carry:-
   130 rounds S.A.A.
    1 day's ration.
    1 Iron ration.
    Tommy's cooker or 2 candles for cooking purposes.

At halfway halt the following will be
issued:-
  To each man. 1 day's rations.
        50 rounds S.A.A.
        2 Bombs.
        2 Sandbags.
  To each bomber: 12 bombs to be carried in sandbags.
  To each rifle grenadier: 6 rifle grenades, to be
        carried in the pouches.
  (Only 1 bandolier of S.A.A. to be carried by
   Rifle Grenadiers.)
  Every other man of "C", "A" and "B" Companies.
       2 Ground Flares.
  To each Company 50 Very Lights 1" white
        10 S.O.S. rockets.
        20 Picks.
        20 Shovels.

The extra S.A.A. etc will be carried as follows:-
 Two limbers will be allotted to each Company.
   of which (a) contains Lewis guns, Magazines
       and spare parts. Also 6000 S.A.A.
       for the use of rifles, to be issued
       in bandoliers, 1 to each man.

(b) 375 Grenades. M.
 100   "   No 23.
 90 Halls Rifle Grenades
 50 Very Lights
 10 S.O.S Rockets
 30 Picks
 30 Shovels
 150 Flares. (A. C + D Coys only.)
 250 Sandbags.
     Rations for attack - 1 day.

Officers Dress.
 All officers will be dressed and equipped the same as their men.

W.T. Sainsbury
Lieut & Adjt
11th Bn West Yorkshire Regt

APPENDIX "A"
to
OPERATION ORDER No 1.
CONTACT AEROPLANE.

Copy No. 5

Arrangements for communication between advanced troops and aeroplanes will be as follows:-

1. A Contact Aeroplane will be maintained in the air from ZERO (if light enough) till ZERO plus 5 hours 10 minutes.

Aeroplanes of the 10th Corps Squadron are distinguished by three broad white bands on the fuselage and are further distinguished by the attachment of a Black board on the left lower plane.

2. Contact Aeroplanes will call for flares by firing a white light and sounding a Klaxon Horn.

Leading Infantry will light flares approximately at the following time.

On the RED line. - ZERO plus 45 minutes.

Isolated bodies of troops out of touch on their flanks should light flares when called on to do so by aeroplanes.

The colour of flares will be RED.

The lighting of flares should be supplemented by waving helmets, handkerchiefs, maps, papers, mess tins or any light coloured objects.

Troops who display no movement when the aeroplane is over them render themselves liable to be mistaken for the enemy who would thus try to avoid being observed.

Flares should be lit in groups of three or four flares. Care must be taken not to use all the flares at one time.

W.F. Sanister
Lieut & Adj
11th Bn West Yorkshire Regt

Sept. 17th 1917.

BATTLE OF MENIN ROAD

ATTACK BY 23rd DIVISION.

PREPARATION FOR THE ATTACK

C Coy. 11th Bn West Yorkshire Rgt

Certified that the packs of the NCOs & men of the above company have been marked as follows:-

Rank & Name
, Platoon
 Company.

J E Douglas
Lieut.
Commandg 'C' Company
11th Bn West Yorkshire Rgt.

The Field
17/9/04.

To The C.O. 11th Bn. West Yorkshire Regt.

From O.C. B Coy 11th Bn. West Yorkshire Regt.

Certified that all Packs belonging NCO's and men of my Company have been marked with Regimental number, name, platoon, and Company, in accordance with your memo A9/55 d/17-9-17

B.H. Saunders Capt
O.C. B Coy
11th Bn West Yorks Regt.

17.9.17

D Coy 1st West Yorks Regt
1/9/14

To Adjt 1st West Yorks.

Certified that the clothing of
N.C.Os & men of D Coy 1st W.Y.R.
are marked in the required manner
re Owing to Rank & Name.
Platoon
Company.

C B Armstrong
Capt
O.C. D Coy 1st W.Y.R.

"A" Form.
MESSAGES AND SIGNALS.

Army Form C.2121 (in pads of 100).

Prefix ...... Code ...... m. Office of Origin and Service Instructions.	Words / Charge	This message is on a/c of: .... Service. (Signature of "Franking Officer.")	Recd. at .... m. Date .... From .... By ....
	Sent At .... m. To By		

TO {

Sender's Number.	Day of Month.	In reply to Number.		
*	18		•	A A A

Actual Casualties. Sept 18th to E. Офрм.

"A" Coy	2	Killed	6	Wounded
"B" Coy	1	"	1	"
"C" Coy	2	"	8	"
"D" Coy	1	"	1	"
H.Q.			3	

Noon 18th to Noon 19th — 5 Killed — 118 Wounded

From
Place
Time

Action

H.Q. CABLE.

List of Dead Buried.

Coy.	A (Own Units)	B (Other Units)	C (Enemy)
"A"	5	33	9.
"D"	–	7	19.
Total	5.	40	28.

(Copy)

O.C. 11th W. Yorks. R.

Total estimated casualties for your unit for
period 19/9/17 to 22/9/17 as follows

Officers   O.R.
   7   300

M Wehle
Capt.
Staff Captain
69th Inf Bde.

O.C. 11th W. Yorks.

Following are total numbers of all ranks (including officers) of your unit admitted to hospital up to noon 22nd inst.

157 (1 attd. from 6th D.of)

A.W.Roberts
Capt.
Staff Captn.
69th Inf. Bde.

> H.Q.,
> 69TH INFANTRY BDE.
> No. ....
> Date. ....

O.C. 11th W. Yorks.
    8th Yorks.
    9th Yorks.
    10th D. of W.
    69th M.G.C.
    69th T.M.B. O.C. Bde. Reinforcement Camp.

Estimated casualties as follows:

	Offrs.	O.R.
11th W. Yorks.	6	150
9th Yorks.	10	200
10th Duke of Well.	5	200
69th M.G.C.	1	8
69th T.M.B.	2	20

No report to hand from 8th Yorks R.

                Capt.
                Staff Capt.
                69th Inf. Bde.

"A" Form.
MESSAGES AND SIGNALS.

Army Form C. 2121.
(In pads of 100.)

Copy

TO: Headquarters 69th Inf Bde.

Sender's Number.	Day of Month.	In reply to Number.	AAA
A 9/101	86	M 8888	

Action Casualties; as called for in your M8888 of 85. inst.

Officers.	Killed	2
	Died of wounds	8
	Wounded	8 ※
	Wounded (at Duty)	2
		8

※ Includes Medical Officer (RAMC. att. this Unit)

O.Rs.	Killed	55
	Died of wounds	6
	Wounded	207
	Wounded (at duty)	3
	Missing	11
		282

Lieut & Adjt
11 W. Yorks

B Coy 11th Bn West Yorks Regt.
List of Casualties

Reg No	Rank	Name	Killed	Wounded	Missing
235656	Pte	Lawlor T C	✓	20/9/17	
41112	"	Burnett E B	✓	20/9/17	
9354	Corpl	Young A G	✓	20/9/17	
13932	Pte	Freeman T	✓	20/9/17	
1576	"	Tate S	✓	20/9/17	
41119	"	Toby B	✓	20/9/17	
20513	"	Ellis W	✓	19/9/17	
29261	"	Walker E	✓	19/9/17	
1638	"	Morris T M	✓	20/9/17	
41142	Pte	Harrison J	✓	20/9/17	
22184	"	Chapman R G	✓	20/9/17	
41135	Pte	Mowson S	✓	20/9/17	
41152	"	Haywood A	✓	20/9/17	
23566	"	Bird J B	✓	20/9/17	
37220	"	Bradley K	✓	20/9/17	
235664	"	Tuckman E	✓	20/9/17	

Reg No	Rank	Name	Killed	Wounded	Missing
3130a	Pte	Alderson G ✓		20/9/17	
30736	"	Whitehead E ✓		18/9/17	
30762S	"	Wilson JW ✓		20/9/17	
29760	"	Coates W ✓		18/9/17	
13912	L/c	Harley R ✓		20/9/17	
235380	Pte	Reed JR ✓		20/9/17	
41138	"	Price G ✓		23/9/17	
8712	Sgt	Saunders W ✓		20/9/17	
34057	Pte	Fairley EH ✓		20/9/17	
267592	"	Thornton E ✓		20/9/17	
13960	C/S	Moore M ✓		20/9/17	
41448	Pte	Cohen S ✓		20/9/17	
17520	"	Hardman H ✓		20/9/17	
23565	"	Stinnes AC ✓		20/9/17	
103	L/C	Gregory JP ✓		20/9/17	
12140	Sgt	Piper WH ✓		18/9/17	
8394	Cpl	Sterell T ✓		18/9/17	
23523	"	Tirrell C ✓		18/9/17	

Reg No	Rank	Name	Killed	Wounded	Missing
6151	L/c	Knigston W	✓	20/9/17	
13235	C/c	Banks F	✓	18/9/17	
10205	"	Beark O	✓	20/9/17	
21698	"	Beach W	✓	20/9/17	
13869	"	Tucker J	✓	18/9/17	
268390	"	Myers G	✓	20/9/17	
25079	"	Davy J	✓	20/9/17	
307147	"	Kentish H	✓	20/9/17	
265369	"	Herbertson P	✓	18/9/17	
307549	"	Devries J	✓	20/9/17	
201625	"	Rev E H	✓	18/9/17	
15079	L/c	Hartley GH	✓	20/9/17	
10662	"	Mitchell K	✓	20/9/17	
1190	Sergt	Weston H	✓	20/9/17	
8534	Corpl	Neoblij C	✓	20/9/17	
M.0680	P/c	Stinford E	Died of wounds 21/9/17	20/9/17	
32632	"	Clough A J	✓	18/9/17	
2/497	"	Bentley A	✓	20/9/17	

R.P.	Rank	Name	Killed	Wounded	Missing
37282	Pte	Garwood C.W	✓	18/9/17	
37759	"	Mackray W	✓	18/9/17	
235566	"	Farmer T	✓	20.9.17	
41151	"	Garritt A	✓	4.9.17	
307204	"	Murphy E.J	✓	20.9.17	
14436	"	Taunah D	✓	20.9.17	
235378	"	Astley T	✓	20/9/17	

11/9/17

9

A. Wood Capt OC B Coy
11th West Yorks Reg.

Own Pln	1	39	1	Total
	16		11	59

Action

To Adjutant
11th West Yorks R^t

C. in (LIGHT) TRENCH MORTAR BATTERY.
No. 5143
Date 25-9-17

Casualty Report

Missing bel'd Killed

N° 13615 Pte Walworth F.W. 20-9-17

Wounded
N° 8001 L/Cpl Hirst F. 21-9-17
· 43716 Pte Everett J. 20-9-17
· 12958 · Lister A. 20-9-17
· 306446 · Mawson A. 20-9-17

Attached men

Killed
N° 24689 Pte James G. 20-9-17

Missing bel'd Killed
N° 15619 Pte Clarkson J.A. 20-9-17

Wounded
N° 202516 Pte Smith A. 20-9-17

J.R. Gibson Lt
for O.C. 69 T.M.B

A Company Casualty Report 25/9/17

No	Rank	Name	Nature of Casualty	Date
14775	Sgt	Lynch J	Wounded	18.9.17
8865		Frost A	Wounded	18.9.17
325051	Pte	Broadbent A	Killed	18.9.17
14588		Poole D	Wounded	18.9.17
15609		Kinley WG	Wounded	18.9.17
25176	Cpl	Russell HP	Killed	20.9.17
12010		Pulford JW	Wounded	20.9.17
18/1574		Butterworth A	Killed	20.9.17
16/1636	L/C	Barker JR	Wounded	20.9.17
305873	Pte	Alderson R	Wounded	20.9.17
51408		Baxter RG	Wounded	20.9.17
~~325051~~		~~Broadbent A~~	~~Killed~~	~~18~~
37299		Carr A	Wounded	20.9.17
266085		Callam B	Wounded	
13435	Cpl	Harrison A	Wounded	20.9.17
28424	Pte	Darby C	Wounded	20.9.17
18/1421		Greenwood R	Wounded	18.9.17
16/1600		Hodgson H	Wounded	20.9.17
19351		Rach A	Wounded	20.9.17
51428		Pride H	Wounded	18.9.17
41491		Towse E	Wounded	20.9.17
16090		Wort J	Wounded	20.9.17
14777		Wright H	Wounded	18.9.17
265209		Walker G	Killed	18.9.17
21348	L/C	Brown J	Killed	20.9.17
57406	Pte	Adamson	Wounded	23.9.17
200692		Boyes E	Wounded	19.9.17

K5 WD1

No	Rank and Name	Nature of Casualty	Date of Casualty
28798	Pte Rest W	Killed	20.9.17
57413	" Brown W	Killed	19.9.17
306085	" Barnes E	Wounded	19.9.17
235593	" Cartwright J.W.	Wounded	20.9.17
57415	" Curwen J.	Killed	20.9.17
200327	" Drever A.	Wounded	20.9.17
303853	" Greaves W.	Killed	19.9.17
267323	" Hodges S	Wounded	20.9.17
202210	" Lawson E	Wounded	19.9.17
57421	" Morris A.O.	Wounded	20.9.17
57424	" Newton A	Wounded	23.9.17
262260	" Rees L	Missing	none
36616	" Sloman W	Wounded	20.9.17
200318	" Trousdale A.	Wounded	20.9.17
8245	Cpl Morgan J.W.	Wounded	20.9.17
8365	L/Sgt Quinlan M	Wounded	20.9.17
		Rejoined	22.9.17
41106	Pte Bartlam L	Wounded	19.9.17
57411	" Blackburn W.P.	Wounded	20.9.17
14613	" Cameron J	Killed	20.9.17
268062	" Dean R.C.	Missing	
28027	" Emsley D.J.	Killed	20.9.17
513	" Kennedy J	Wounded	21.9.17
305475	" Snows Jn°	Killed	20.9.17
16187	" Syres E.	Missing	
14671	Sgt Soothill W.	Wounded	20.9.17
43721	Cpl Kitson C	Wounded	20.9.17
37371	L/Cpl Ash J	Wounded	20.9.17
41117	" Barraclough W	Wounded	20.9.17
		Rejoined	21.9.17

K.7. W.16. Wounded 2. Missing 2.

No.	Rank & Name		Nature Casualty	Date of Casualty
57425	Pte	Nolan G.J.	Wounded	23.9.17
235589	"	Seager H.E.	Killed	20.9.17
18793	"	Thompson A.	Wounded	20.9.17
13198	"	Fox C.R.	Missing	Rejoined
265636	"	Wood C.	Wounded	20.9.17
306688	"	Wood C.R.	Missing	
9549	"	Hemsby J.	Missing	
57407	"	Ayers A.	Wounded	
307576	"	Stott W.	Wounded	
15412	"	Devanney J.	Wounded	
57409	"	Bindoff L.F.	Wounded	
13626	"	Bromley N.	Wounded	20.9.17
200177	"	Ralston R.A.	Wounded	20.9.17
235586	"	Savage R.P.	Killed	20.9.17
15979	"	Howard E.	Wounded	20.9.17
14593	L/C	Glynn M.	Wounded	
14032	"	Sykes W.	Wounded	20.9.17
41123	Pte	Anderson W.	Wounded	
16449	"	Jones C.	Wounded	
41114	"	Snape E.J.	Killed	
29693	"	Whiteley L.	Missing	

K 3 W 14 Missing 4

Killed	Wounded	Wnd.Duty	Missing
15	51	2	6

74

C. Coy. 11th West Yorks Regt. 25.9.17

Casualties in action f. 20.9.17

Reg. No.	Rank	Name	Nature of Casualty	Date of Casualty	Remarks
43769	Pte	Wild J.	Killed	20.9.17	
14356	"	Brown F.	Do.	20.9.17	
37822	"	Bradley C.	Do.	22.9.17	
11125	"	Gibson H.	Do.	20.9.17	
265304	"	Marwood J.	Do.	19.9.17	
42757	"	Pratt J. J.	Do.	20.9.17	
42759	"	Gibson J. W.	Do.	20.9.17	
10293	"	Ness R.	Do.	20.9.17	
267321	"	Smithson F.L.	Do.	20.9.17	
14859	Cpl	Cotter J. E.	Do.	20.9.17	
42768	Pte	Potts R.	Do.	20.9.17	
42749	"	Baston J. T.	Do.	20.9.17	
14192	L/Cpl	Moso R.	Do.	20.9.17	
14514	Pte	Barford W.	Do.	20.9.17	
13713	Cpl	Davies J. L.	Died of Wounds	19.9.17	K 14
14518	L/Cpl	Harris B.	Do	19.9.17	D/W 2
10476	Pte	Brooke G.	Wounded	18.9.17	
267947		Dickinson F.	Do	20.9.17	W 9
268664		Holt W.	Do	20.9.17	/30
306787		Roddings W.	Do	20.9.17	
153624		Simms A. B.	Do	20.9.17	
13712		Kent F.	Do	20.9.17	
1820	L/Cpl	Clay C.	Do.	20.9.17	
47208	Pte	Bickford J.	Do	22.9.17	
42766		Martin R.	Do	20.9.17	

C. Coy. 11th West Yorkshire Regt.   25.9.17.

Casualties in action of 20.9.17. Contd.

Reg No	Rank	Name	Nature of Casualty	Date of Casualty	Remarks
42748	Pte	Bowler A.G.T.	Wounded	20.9.17	
42747		Alder H.R.	Killed	20.9.17	
42752		Cairns J.	Wounded	20.9.17	K1
42760		Geldert J.	Do.	20.9.17	
12990	Sgt	Riley H.	Do.	19.9.17	L/B
14353	L/Cpl	Clifton T.	Do.	18.9.17	
43883	Sgt	Sparks W.A.	Do.	20.9.17	W
18007	L/Cpl	Fearn G.	Do.	18.9.17	
37301	Pte	Coombes C.T.	Do.	20.9.17	
223325	-	Potter H.	Do.	18.9.17	
41222	-	Wright H.	Do.	20.9.17	
265187	-	Swainson H.	Do.	20.9.17	
267275	L/Cpl	Thorpe R.	Do.	18.9.17	
17/612	Pte	Hill A.	Do.	20.9.17	
42758		Forster J.	Do.	18.9.17	
42759		Gibson J.T.			
24833		Dennis J.	Do.	19.9.17	
41202		Warden F.	Do.	19.9.17	
37398	Cpl	Bulmer C.	Do.	20.9.17	
13788	Pte	Norris E.	Do.	19.9.17	
268255		Eccles J.	Do.	19.9.17	
305272		Calverley T.	Do.	19.9.17	
306429		Miller H.	Do.	19.9.17	H.Q.
265387		Hutchinson R.	Do.	18.9.17	
47289		Appleby G.W.	Do.	19.9.17	

C. Coy. 11th West Yorks. Regt.   25-9-17.

Casualties in action of 20-9-17. Contd.

Reg No	Rank	Name	Nature of Casualty	Date of Casualty	Remarks
22421	Pte	Carr H. B.	Wounded	19-9-17	
18978		Wardle F.	Do	19-9-17	
340141		Jackson J. W.	Do	19-9-17	
18065		Horley L. M.	Do	19-9-17	Rejoined 26/9/17
25930		Gill S.	Do	19-9-17	
23942		Gallagher CA	Do	20-9-17	
23939		Wright F.	Do	19-9-17	
42746		Allan R.	Do	20-9-17	
354445		Cawdrey C.	Do	19-9-17	No 83
411243		Worsley R.	Do	20-9-17	DyW 1/W
1536	Sgt	Marshall H.	Do	20-9-17	
14612	-	Turpin E.	Do	20-9-17	
7556	Cpl	Furness E.	Do	20-9-17	
143140	L/Cpl	Gore F.	Do	21-9-17	
13437	Pte	Lonsdale A.	Do	20-9-17	
37044		Raine W.	Do	20-9-17	
37193		Hyde J.	Do	23-9-17	
8296		Muir J. W.	Do	20-9-17	
76186		Knipe H.	Do	20-9-17	
39449		Exley P.	Do	20-9-17	
7834		Usher A. M.	Do	20-9-17	
39729		Marshall E.	Died of wounds	22-9-17	
~~34444~~					
267796		Ridge A.	Wounded Do	20-9-17	
1504		Sanderson H.	Do	20-9-17	

C. Coy. 11th West Yorks. Regt.   25.9.17.
Casualties in action of 20.9.17.   Contd.

Reg No	Rank	Name	Nature of Casualty	Date of Casualty	Remarks
25165	Pte	Shirley J.W.	Wounded	20.9.17	
36825		Galloway W.	Do	20.9.17	
42772		Samuels P.	Do.	21.9.17	
266416		Collett W.	Do	20.9.17	Rejoined 23.9.17.
18175		Hanson B.	Do.	20.9.17	
16/1596		Steele W.	Do.	20.9.17	
~~		~~Anderson H.~~	~~Do~~	~~20.9.17~~	Attached from A. Coy
14370	Pte	Doody H.	Missing	20.9.17	
39499	-	Carroll W.	Do.	20.9.17	
244494	-	Hainsworth C.A.	Wounded	20.9.17	
305845	-	Wood A.	Missing	20.9.17	
42762	-	Henzell J.	Killed	19.9.17	
32197	-	Taylor H.	Missing	20.9.17	
15830	Sgt	Bell A.H.	Wounded	20.9.17	
15645	Pte	Emery T.	Do.	20.9.17	
14792	-	Middleton R.	Do	20.9.17	
15653	-	Newman G.	Do	18.9.17	1.K.
14558	-	Robinson E.	Do.		1W
15/1940	-	Sunley J.	Do.		
17865	Cpl	Farrell J.	Do.	22.9.17	1 Wounded

D.W. 3.

K.	W.	Wounded at Duty	Missing		
16	69	1	4	NB	90

Action /

Burials

Regt. No.	Rank.	Name.	Regt.
41114	Pte.	Snape E.J.	11th West Yk. R.
41156	Pte.	Caithness R.	11th West Yk. R.

30th Sept. 1917.

C R Armstrong Captain
for Staff Captain
69th Inf. Bde.

THE ATTACK IN PROGRESS

"C" Form.
MESSAGES AND SIGNALS.

Army Form C. 2123.
(In books of 100.)

Prefix: FCR
Service Instructions: LOA

TO: OC Sind

*Sender's Number	Day of Month	In reply to Number	AAA
BM 476	21st		

Following from army to corps commander aaa Please accept and convey to your division my heartiest congratulations on fresh success achieved today

FROM PLACE & TIME: Cable

"A" Form.
MESSAGES AND SIGNALS.

Army Form C. 2121.
(In pads of 100.)

No. of Message ....

Prefix .... Code .... m	Words.	Charge.	This message is on a/c of:	Recd. at ...... m.
Office of Origin and Service Instructions.	Sent			Date ......
	At ...... m.		.... Service.	From ......
	To			
	By	(Sig. of "Franking Officer.")	By ......

TO { O.C. Sand. ~~Clay. Stone. Granite.~~ Hay ~~String.~~

Sender's Number	Day of Month	In reply to Number	
* B.G.7.	21st.		AAA

The following from Divisional Commander to
Brigadier begins well done I knew the 69th
~~would do real well and congratulate you heart-~~
~~ily on excellent results.~~ I cannot be more
proud of your work then I always have been
and I hope to tell you all so shortly. Ends.
~~G.O.C. 2nd Anzac Brigade has also sent his~~
~~congratulations and has expressed his pleasure~~
~~in the manner we worked together.~~

From Cable.
Place
Time

The above may be forwarded as now corrected. (Z)

Brig. Genl.

Censor.   Sig. of Addressor or person authorised to telegraph in his name.

"A" Form.
MESSAGES AND SIGNALS.

Army Form C. 2121.
(In pads of 100.)

No. of Message..........

Prefix......... Code......... m	Words.	Charge.	This message is on a/c of:	Recd. at....... m
Office of Origin and Service Instructions.	Sent		..........Service.	Date......
....	At.........m.			From......
....	To........			
	By.......		(Sig. of "Franking Officer.")	By......

TO { O.C. Sand / Clay. Stone. Granite.
      Hay   String.

Sender's Number	Day of Month	In reply to Number	
* E.M.493.	24th.		AAA

Following from Second Army AAA The
Commander - in - Chief has received the
following message from Field Marshall
Viscount FRENCH AAA

Begins AAA My warmest congratulations
and best wishes to you and all my old
comrades AAA The Commander - in - Chief
has sent on this message to the Army
Commander who hopes you will communicate
it to the troops under your command. AAA
E N D S AAA

[signature]
Capt.,
Brigade Major.

From C A B L E.
Place
Time

The above may be forwarded as now corrected.   (Z)

....
    Censor.   Sig. of Addressor or person authorised to telegraph in his name.

* This line should be erased if not required.
(27964) Wt. W492/M1647. [E 1187]. 130,000 Pads—5/17. M.R.Co.,Ltd Forms/C.2121

"A" Form.
MESSAGES AND SIGNALS.

Army Form C. 2121
(in pads of 100).
No of Message..........

Prefix........ Code........ m	Words	Charge	This message is on a/c of:	Recd. at........... m
Office of Origin and Service Instructions.	Sent		...........................Service.	Date...............
....	At............ m			From.............
....	To............		(Signature of "Franking Officer.")	By...............
....	By............			

TO { Lieut C. Durham

Sender's Number.	Day of Month.	In reply to Number.	AAA
*FR546	20		

Our right Coy. is disposed
as under: Front
Platoon posts at
J.14.D.5.9, J.14.B.6.4, J.14.D.15.95
(Coy Hdqrs.) J.14.B.4.4 aaa
All Bn objectives consolidated aaa
are now being heavily shelled

From
Place
Time 1130

The above may be forwarded as now corrected.

Censor.   Signature of Addressee or person authorised to telegraph in his name.
* This line should be erased if not required.

"G" Form.
MESSAGES AND SIGNALS.

Army Form C. 2123
(In books of 100.)

Prefix **NB** Code **14A** Words **15**
Received From **R3** By **Carly**
Service Instructions **R3**

TO **Cable**

Sender's Number	Day of Month	In reply to Number	AAA
R4	20		

Stone have gained 2nd
objective aaa Granite attacking
green line

FROM **Sand**
TIME & PLACE **9.49 AM**

"C" Form.
MESSAGES AND SIGNALS.

Army Form C. 2123.
(In books of 100.)

No. of Message..........

Prefix.... Code.... Words....	Received.	Sent, or sent out.	Office Stamp
£ s. d.	From........	At........'m.	
Charges to Collect	By........	To........	
Service Instructions		By........	

Handed in at.......... Office.......m. Received.......m.

TO

*Sender's Number	Day of Month	In reply to Number	AAA

Counter attack imminent
Prisoners coming in in
Hundreds in all directions
the own detcht of C Coy
but Coy has been sent by
Young well away on
left apparent 2 or 3 batns
& Platoons of B Coy

FROM
PLACE & TIME

*This line should be erased if not required.

"C" Form.
MESSAGES AND SIGNALS.

Army Form C. 2123.
(In books of 100.)

No. of Message............

Prefix	Code	Words	Received	Sent, or sent out.	Office Stamp
	£ s. d.		From.........	At.........m.	
Charges to Collect			By.........	To.........	
Service Instructions				By.........	

Handed in at .... Office ....m. Received ....m.

TO

*Sender's Number	Day of Month	In reply to Number	AAA
reached Red Line & fill			
~~gap~~ ~~Coy moving to~~			
gap & take over.			
All going top hole			
Enemy M.G. them is			
tank trap			
		L[ieu]t. H[...]	
			2nd L[t]

FROM
PLACE & TIME

*This line should be erased if not required.

"C" Form.
MESSAGES AND SIGNALS.

Army Form C. 2123.
(In books of 100.)

Capt. Saunders reports what appears to be heavy enemy counter attack over Dumbarton Lakes. Several Hundred prisoners coming in down Menin Road.

L.L.S.

"C" Form.
MESSAGES AND SIGNALS.

Army Form C. 2123.
(In books of 100.)

Prefix **XB** Code **AKA** Words **15**

Service Instructions: **R-3**

Sent, or sent out. At **9.53 A**m. To **LOC** By **S/Rsck**

TO Cable

*Sender's Number	Day of Month	In reply to Number	AAA
R-4	20		

9th	Yorks	have	gained
2nd	Objective	West	Riding
attacking		Green	Line
			9-49
			from Fifth

FROM PLACE & TIME: **2nd 9-49 AM**

"C" Form.
MESSAGES AND SIGNALS.

Army Form C. 2123
(In books of 100.)

Prefix **SB** Code...... Words......

By **Partry**

TO **Land**

Sender's Number	Day of Month	In reply to Number	AAA
C Coy has objective is in touch on right and left aaa Detailed note from OC Coy being brought by stretcher bearers			
		9.15 am	

FROM: **B3**

MESSAGES AND SIGNALS.

TO: CABLE

Sender's Number: W5
Day of Month: 20

Capt Saunders reports what appears to be heavy enemy counter attack over Dumbarton Lakes. Also several hundred prisoners coming in down MENIN Road.

"C" Form.
MESSAGES AND SIGNALS.

Army Form C. 2123 (In books of 100.)

Prefix **SB** Code........ Words..........

Received. From **R3** By **W. Wilson**

Sent, or sent out. At...........m. To........... By...........

Office Stamp. **LOC 20/9/17**

Charges to Collect
Service Instructions.

Handed in at............................Office...........m. Received...........m.

TO **SAND**

*Sender's Number	Day of Month	In reply to Number	AAA
No	message	from	coys
yet	german	barrage	very
slight	there	two	tanks
going	up	MENIN	road
from	reports	of	TMB
men	troops	appear to	
be	progressing	satisfactorily	
Prisoners	coming	in	
	6·35 am		

FROM
TIME & PLACE

*This line should be erased if not required

"C" Form.
MESSAGES AND SIGNALS.

Army Form C. 2123
(In books of 100.)

Received. From: B.3 By: H Wallace

Office Stamp: 20/9/17 A.V.

TO Sand

Day of Month: 20th

			AAA
SOE	Going	over	aaa
Too	misty	for	observation
aaa	all	apparently	going
well	aaa	about	20 Prisoners
of	passing	through	a
Coys	line		
	Received	7.5 am	

FROM: B 3

"C" Form.
MESSAGES AND SIGNALS.

Army Form C. 2123
(In books of 100.)

No. of Messages _____

Prefix......Code......Words......	Received.	Sent, or sent out.	Office Stamp
£ s d	From............	At............m.	
Charges to Collect	By............	To............	
Service Instructions.		By............	

Handed in at............Office......... m. Received............

TO Sand

*Sender's Number	Day of Month	In reply to Number	AAA

Australians going for ward well on left. 1000 yds Half left aaa baker wounded in ~~leda~~ aaa Two guns TmB with crews wiped out on ~~chofer~~ Copse apparaching tank trap aaa ~~office~~ killed aaa Rushton TmB wounded

FROM
TIME & PLACE   B3   7.20 am

*This line should be erased if not required

"C" Form.
MESSAGES AND SIGNALS.

Army Form C. 2123
(In books of 100.)

Prefix 56

TO	Sand

Cannot get line through get aaa German Barrage too Heavy will get through as soon as possible aaa line beaten but blown to bits

7.27 a.m.

FROM TIME & PLACE Sig R 3

TO	HEADQUARTERS of

No.	Date	PIGEON SERVICE.
1	20	

No messages yet received from Corps. German barrage very slight in the COPSE. Two tanks going up the MENIN ROAD. Troops appear to be progressing satisfactorily. Prisoners coming in.

FROM	SAND
TIME	6.40 a.m.
PLACE	HQ

No. of copies sent by PIGEON SERVICE.	SENDER'S SIGNATURE
2	T. Sainsbury

TIME of RECEIPT at LOFT.

HEADQUARTERS of

TO | CABLE

Army Book 418.

No.	Date
2	20

PIGEON SERVICE

LOE going past Red Line.

Too misty for much observation.

All apparently going well.

Australians also passing Red Line.

FROM	SAND
PLACE	HQ
TIME	1.15 p.m.

Sender's Signature: W T Sainsbury

HEADQUARTERS of

TO: CABLE

Army Book 418.

No.	Date	PIGEON SERVICE
3	20	

Right Coy reports "all objectives gained. Has begun consolidation. Is in touch with A Coy on left. Is not in touch on right. To date few casualties. Hostile M.G. active on right front of A Coy.

FROM	SAND		
PLACE	HQ	TIME	a.m. / p.m.
Sender's Signature	Lt Sainsbury		
Time of Receipt at Loft		No. of Copies sent by P.S.	2

Army Book 418.

HEADQUARTERS of
TO | CABLE

No.	Date	PIGEON SERVICE
4	20	

<u>Left Coy</u> consolidating in front of Red Line at FITZCLARENCE FARM.

<u>Centre Coy</u> OK & consolidating Red Line. Capt TOWN reported killed.

<u>Right Coy</u>.

Aid Post captured and garrison of HERENTHAGE Chateau surrounded. In touch with N.F's at Herenthage Chateau.

FROM	SAND		
PLACE	H.Q.	TIME	8.17 a.m.
Sender's Signature	Lt Savisby Lb		
Time of Receipt at Loft		No. of Copies sent by P.S.	2

"C" Form.
MESSAGES AND SIGNALS.

Army Form C. 2123
(In books of 100.)

Prefix SA Code...... Words.......	Received. From...... By......	Sent, or sent out. At......m. To...... By......	Office Stamp.
Charges to Collect			
Service Instructions.			

Handed in at.................Office........m. Received.......m

TO

*Sender's Number	Day of Month	In reply to Number	AAA
	20		

2/T ERVING is in possesion with the left of tank trap following message from D Coy aaa Half gained objectives and am consolidating and am in touch with a Coy on left am nofin touch on right aaa To date few casualties Hostile MG active a coy rightfront

FROM TIME & PLACE

17.45

Army Form W. 3431.
MESSAGE PAD.
...... DIVISION.

Map reference
or Mark on Map
at back.

1. I am at ...Objectives......... { and am consolidating.
   ~~and have consolidated.~~
2. I am held up by M.G. at ....
3. I need :— ~~Ammunition.~~ | Water and rations.
   ~~Bombs.~~ | Very lights.
   ~~Rifle bombs.~~ | Stokes shells.
4. Counter attack forming up at ....
5. I am in touch with .....A........ on ~~Right~~ Left at ...Left...
6. I am not in touch on Right / ~~Left~~
7. Am being shelled from ....
8. Present strength ...two Coys Officers... rifles. Reinforcements required :—
   ....Platoons. | ....Sections rifle bombers.
   ....Sections riflemen. | .... ,, Lewis gunners.
   .... ,, bombers.
9. Hostile ... { ~~Battery~~ / Machine Gun / ~~Trench Mortar~~ } active at ...A Coy right front...

Time ...6.15 A.. m.   Name ...R.L. Armstrong Capt...
Date ...26-7-7...   Platoon ....
                         Company ....D................
                         Battalion ...S.A.I.N.........

W1843—R 643 150,000 5/17 HWV(P740)

Army Form W. 3431.
MESSAGE PAD.
......DIVISION.

Map reference
or Mark *on Map*
at back.

1. I am at......Aid Post............ { and am consolidating.
   ~~and have consolidated.~~
2. ~~I am held up by M.G. at~~ ....
3. I need :— ~~Ammunition.~~ | ~~Water and rations.~~
             ~~Bombs.~~ | ~~Very lights.~~
             ~~Rifle bombs.~~ | ~~Stokes shells.~~
4. Counter attack forming up at ....
5. I am in touch with...A & N F....on Right at ...H Q Lat
                                     ~~Left~~
6. ~~I am not in touch on Right~~
                        ~~Left~~
7. Am being shelled from.......back......
8. Present strength...........rifles. Reinforcements required :—
   ....Platoons. | ....Sections rifle bombers.
   ....Sections riflemen. | .... „ Lewis gunners.
   ....   „   bombers. |
9. Hostile ... { Battery
               { Machine Gun   } active at..................
               { Trench Mortar
Time...7.15 A. m.   Name..........................
Date...20-9-17...   Platoon........................
                     Company.......................
                     Battalion......................

W1843—R1643 150,000 5/17 HWV(P740)

We got our objectives
easily but hopelessly
disorganised. Very few
men here but not many
casualties.

4 do have gone through
of Platoon N.F.

Own pipeline barrage
very short
Town killed
Gawe hit
Self hit but staying

Chilmston

"A" Form. MESSAGES AND SIGNALS.

Army Form C.2121 (in pads of 100).

Following Message from D Coy aaa Am at Aid Post aaa Am in touch with A Coy and N.F. at Herenthage Chateau. Am being shelled from back. Orderly "D" Coy reports Herenthage Chateau Demolished with Garrison roughly 50. Also reports Capt Town killed by Shell

From 8/10

"C" Form
MESSAGES AND SIGNALS.

Army Form C. 2123
(In books of 100.)

Prefix **JB** Code........ Words........

Charges to Collect		
Service Instructions.		

Received.
From..................
By.....................

Sent, or sent out.
At................m.
To...............
By.................

Office Stamp.

Handed in at............ Office......... m. Received............ m.

TO ~~Ham Cy 18 adyt~~
A D J Band - Cy 120

*Sender's Number	Day of Month	In reply to Number	AAA
Have	consolidated	on	
RED	LINE	every	thing
OK	I am	very	Slightly
wounded - ~~Bar~~			
	8 20		

FROM BARRACLOUGH

TIME & PLACE

*This line should be erased if not required

"C" Form.
MESSAGES AND SIGNALS.

Army Form C. 2123
(In books of 100.)

Prefix **SB** Code....... Words **18**

Service Instructions: **PRIORITY**

TO Adjt Sand

Sender's Number: **C3**
Day of Month: **20**

Am in touch on both flanks capt town missing Have taken command

8.30

FROM BARRACLOUGH

To SAND

Have dispatched (repeat) message by wire. Approximate position as in sketch map attached.
Thomas + most of his platoon not here, seem to have strayed somewhere. 3 offrs + about 60 OR. at present.

Nearest post to ANZAC 5 about 20 yds, to A Coy about 40 yds. Have 3 L.G. here one being a Coy's.

Bosche MG firing from direction of SW corner of Polygon Wood. Can do with water at any first convenient moment. also MG ammⁿ

Tower
□

ANZABS — — ※ — — — ※ — — A coy
                    ↓
              Coy HQ connected by wire
              to SANDS two Ridings

"C" Form.
MESSAGES AND SIGNALS.

Army Form C. 2123

Prefix S.5

Sent: To Wallace

TO **Sand**

Capt Clarkson reports Lt Douglas digging 120 yds in front of Red line ~~all~~ our objective taken

8.20

FROM / TIME & PLACE: R3

"C" Form
MESSAGES AND SIGNALS.

Army Form C. 2123
(In books of 100.)

Prefix: SB Words: 44

Service Instructions: PRIOR

TO: ADJT Sand

Sender's Number	Day of Month	In reply to Number	AAA
C2	20		

Captured and am consolidating J14D 9.6 to J14D 9.8 aaa Can bring covering fire to protect A Coy and also ANZACS. Coy HQ dugout at one hundred yards west of tower J14D 9960 aaa Have at present about 60 men

8.30

FROM TIME & PLACE: OC D & C Coy

Casualties.

D. Company   11TH (S.) BATT. WEST YORKSHIRE REGT.

BATTLE CASUALTIES
During Operations Sept. 18th To —24"

Regt. No.	Rank	Name		Nature Casualty	Date		
13294	CSM	Albrighton	A	Killed	20	9	17
8952	Sergt	Cass	J	Died of Wounds	22	9	17
12155	LCpl	Harrison	J	Killed	20	9	17
36097	"	Kemp	CS	Killed	20	9	17
13364	"	Upton	E	Killed	20	9	17
1707	Pte	Oakes	HL	Killed	20	9	17
267975	"	Kendall	JL	Killed	20	9	17
15843	"	Arnold	W	Killed	20	9	17
18/1405	"	Crossland	H	Died of Wounds			
41156	"	Caithness	R	Killed	21	9	17
7230	Corpl	Carroll	P	Wounded	20	9	17
11346	"	Potts	W	Wounded	20	9	17
16/1516	Sergt	Scott	SA	Wounded	20	9	17
15818	Corpl	Speight	E	Wounded	20	9	17
1755	"	Whitley	JJ	Wounded	20	9	17
13576	LCpl	Taylor	W	Wounded	20	9	17
12639	"	Woodcock	J	Wounded	20	9	17
13092	Pte	Brammer	J	Wounded	20	9	17
15852	"	Belcher	S	Wounded	20	9	17
15137	"	Beasley	T.v B	Wounded	20	9	17
41195	"	Barker	J	Wounded	20	9	17
14726	"	Clarkson	W	Wounded	20	9	17
28038	"	Catterick	W	Wounded	20	9	17
235678	"	Crooke	EC	Wounded	20	9	17
305269	"	Fraser	W	Wounded	20	9	17
14539	"	Goodchild	J	Wounded	20	9	17
241448	"	Hill	J	Wounded	20	9	17
37182	"	Hodgson	H	Wounded	20	9	17
34227	"	Hudson	J	Wounded	20	9	17
42665	"	Lawrence	EC	Wounded	20	9	17
19851	"	Lancaster	AJ	Wounded	20	9	17
305126	"	Miller	G	Wounded	20	9	17
12449	"	Milner	J	Wounded	20	9	17
235681	"	Marshall	W	Wounded	20	9	17
13508	"	Pipes	A	Wounded	20	9	17
235695	"	Pinniger	S	Wounded	20	9	17
8942	"	Ryan	JW	Wounded	19	9	17
13104	"	Sykes	E	Wounded	20	9	17
307732	"	Stanton	J	Wounded	20	9	17

REGT. NO	RANK	NAME		NATURE of Casualty	DATE	
242032	Pte	Looby	W.	Wounded	20. 9. 17.	
25456	"	Wilcock	H.	Wounded	20. 9. 17.	
13329	"	Wilson	GH.	Wounded	20. 9. 17.	
12592	"	Wilson	AR.	Wounded	20. 9. 17.	
11689	"	Weathers	JC.	Wounded	20. 9. 17.	
17841	"	Wilson	J.	Wounded	20. 9. 17.	
268056	"	Stephenson	H.	Wounded	20. 9. 17.	
235686	"	Bassett	AJ.	Wounded	20. 9. 17.	
307255	"	Watson	JW.	Wounded	20. 9. 17.	
37960	"	Walker	E.	Wounded	20. 9. 17.	
38259	"	Calvert	J.	Wounded	20. 9. 17.	
32625	"	Metcalf	D.	Wounded	20. 9. 17.	
12732	"	Whiteley	C.	Wounded	21. 9. 17.	
7984	"	Riley	J.	Wounded	20. 9. 17.	
306107	"	Taylor	J.	Wounded	20. 9. 17.	
240791	"	Haley	B.	Wounded	20. 9. 17.	
33228	"	Brook	Jas	Wounded	20. 9. 17.	

56.

C. L. Armstrong
Capt.
O/C C Coy

Killed	Died of wounds	Wounded	Missing
O.R. 8	2	46	nil

Total
Officers nil
O.Rs. 56.

Secret.   Copy No. 14.

OPERATION INSTRUCTIONS
BY
LIEUT-COLONEL P. W. LETHBRIDGE,
COMMANDING 10TH. BATTALION DUKE OF WELLINGTON'S REGIMENT.
++++++++++++++++++++++++

Map References - HOOGE 1/10,000 and TRENCH OPERATION MAP 1/5,000.

1. The 23RD. DIVISION will attack and capture the line J.15.d.40.90 - J.21.b.40.10 - J.21.c.35.75 on a date and at a zero hour to be notified later. The attack will be in conjunction with simultaneous attacks on the whole 2nd. and 5th. Army Fronts.

2. The 69TH. INFANTRY BRIGADE will capture the line J.15.d.40.90 - J.21.b.40.60. The objectives and Brigade and Battalion boundaries are shown on the maps already in possession of O.C. Companies.
   The 2ND. AUSTRALIAN BRIGADE will attack on the LEFT and the 68TH. INFANTRY BRIGADE on the RIGHT, the Battalions of these Brigades detailed for the GREEN LINE being the 8TH. AUSTRALIAN INFANTRY BATTALION and the 13TH. BATTALION DURHAM LIGHT INFANTRY respectively.

3. The 11TH. WEST YORKSHIRE REGIMENT will capture and consolidate Brigade Front on the RED LINE; the 9TH. YORKSHIRE REGIMENT will capture Brigade Front on the BLUE LINE; this Battalion will capture and consolidate the GREEN LINE.

4. The Battalion, plus "D" Company 8TH. YORKSHIRE REGIMENT, will attack the GREEN LINE in two bounds.
   "A" and "B" Companies and two platoons of "D" Coy. 8TH. YORKSHIRE REGIMENT will attack and consolidate a line J.21.a.2.7. - J.15.a.95.00. "A" Coy. will be responsible for all the ground SOUTH of the track running East-South-East through VELDHOEK.
   "B" Coy. will be responsible for all the ground between that last named track and the track running East-South-East SOUTH of NORTHAMPTON FARM.
   "D" Coy. 8TH. YORKSHIRE REGIMENT will be responsible for the remainder of this portion of the Battalion's objective.
   "A" Coy. will commence the construction of STRONG POINT "N" and will construct similar strong points North and South to connect with the 13TH. BATTALION DURHAM LIGHT INFANTRY on the RIGHT and "B" Company on the LEFT.
   "B" Coy. will construct at least two STRONG POINTS about J.15.d.05.30 and J.15.d.0.5.
   "D" Coy. 8TH. YORKSHIRE REGIMENT will commence the construction of STRONG POINT "V" and will make at least one other STRONG POINT to command the VALLEY OF THE REUTELBEEK. This line will form the SUPPORT LINE.
   "C" Coy. will attack the GREEN LINE from the RIGHT BOUNDARY to the DUG OUT at the apex of the German Line at J.15.d.60.35 inclusive.
   "B" Coy. will capture the GREEN LINE from that point to a line between the CENTRE OF THE FOUR GERMAN DUG OUTS at about J.15.d.35.75.
   "D" Coy. 8TH. YORKSHIRE REGIMENT will capture the remainder of the GREEN LINE including the two left German dug outs.
   On completion of the capture of the GREEN LINE "C" and "D" Companies and half company 8TH. YORKSHIRE REGIMENT will consolidate the line - "C" Coy. being responsible for the consolidation from the RIGHT to J.15.d.45.25; "D" Coy. from that point to J.15.d.40.85 including Strong Point "O"; half company 8TH. YORKSHIRE REGIMENT will be responsible for the consolidation of the remainder of the line, including Strong Point "Q".

"D" Coy. DUKE OF WELLINGTON'S REGIMENT will construct STRONG POINT "O" and at least one other STRONG POINT on their RIGHT and LEFT FLANKS to connect with "C" Coy. DUKE OF WELLINGTON'S REGIMENT and "D" Coy. 8TH. YORKSHIRE REGIMENT.
"D" Coy. 8TH. YORKSHIRE REGIMENT will construct STRONG POINT "Q".

"C" Coy. will construct at least two STRONG POINTS - one in front of the BUILDING at about J.15.d.5.1, and another on the RIGHT FLANK to command the egress from the SCHERRIABEEK VALLEY, SOUTH of POLDERHOEK.

All coys. in the FRONT LINE will put out posts in front of the line as close as possible under the barrage.

All the consolidation will be carried out as rapidly as possible in view of the certainty of an early counter attack.

5.   At 1 p.m. on "D" Day, the Battalion will move to RAILWAY DUG OUTS by platoons at 100 yards intervals. Order of March - H.Q., "A", "B", "C" and "D" Coys. At 9.30 p.m. the Battalion will continue its march to its assembly position in the SANCTUARY WOOD AREA by sections at 100 yards intervals. Order of March - H.Q., "A", "B" and "C" Coys, stretcher bearers, police and pioneers, and "D" Coy. The latter will proceed to YEOMANRY POST direct and report to MAJOR GRELLETT, 9TH. YORKSHIRE REGIMENT.

"D" Coy. 9TH. YORKSHIRE REGIMENT and the FORWARD BRIGADE RESERVE COMPANY of the 9TH. YORKSHIRE REGIMENT will proceed direct from their Battalions to the SANCTUARY WOOD AREA to the positions which will be allotted to them later.

The jumping off position of the Battalion and the two coys. of the 9TH. BATTALION YORKSHIRE REGIMENT will be as follows:-

FORWARD BRIGADE RESERVE COMPANY 9TH. YORKSHIRE REGIMENT in NEW CUT TRENCH, N. of Jasper Lane, and JASPER LANE up to INVERNESS COPSE.

"B" Coy. Duke of Wellington's Regt. in NEW CUT TRENCH, S. of Jasper Lane, NEW CUT between JASPER LANE AND JASPER AVENUE.

"A" Coy. Duke of Wellington's Regt. EASTERN END of JASPER AVENUE.

"D" Coy. 9TH. YORKSHIRE REGIMENT, in JASPER LANE between GRID TRENCH and NEW CUT.

"D" Coy. Duke of Wellington's Regt. in LEFT HALF of GRID TRENCH

"C" Coy. Duke of Wellington's Regt. in the REMAINDER of GRID TRENCH up to JASPER AVENUE and up JASPER AVENUE as far as "A" Coy.

"A" & "C" Coys. will time their departure from SANCTUARY WOOD and YEOMANRY POST so as to get into these positions as soon after ZERO + 10 minutes as possible, that being the hour when GRID and NEW CUT TRENCHES will have been evacuated by the 11TH. WEST YORKSHIRE REGIMENT and the 9TH. YORKSHIRE REGIMENT.

The Battalion plus "D" Coy. 9TH. YORKSHIRE REGIMENT will commence the advance for the attack at ZERO + 3 hours, advancing in columns of half platoons in single file and will deploy for the attack. "A" and "B" Coys. Duke of Wellington's Regt. and 2 platoons 9TH. YORKSHIRE REGIMENT in front of the BLUE LINE and "C" and "D" Coys. Duke of Wellington's Regiment and two platoons of "D" Coy. 9TH. YORKS REGIMENT immediately behind the BLUE LINE and will carry on the advance immediately on the barrage going forward at ZERO + 4 hours 13 minutes.

The deployment will be delayed as far forward as possible.

"A" and "C" Coys. will take care not to move SOUTH of JASPER AVENUE in order to give room for the various companies of the 69TH. INFANTRY BRIGADE which are moving through the SOUTHERN portion of the 69TH. INFANTRY BRIGADE AREA.

The artillery and machine gun BARRAGE will be as shown on the barrage maps to all concerned.

6.   The MACHINE GUN OFFICER will arrange to place two of his machine guns at a position immediately to the EAST of STRONG POINT "B" to command the VALLEY OF THE REUTELBEEK. Two guns will be placed on the right flank of the GREEN LINE in a position to command

-3-

the egress from the SCHERRIABEEK VALLEY.

7. The O.i/c.TRENCH MORTARS will place two guns at STRONG POINT "N" and two guns near the HOUSE at J.13.d.15.45.

8. FORWARD BRIGADE SIGNAL STATION and the FORWARD BATTALION SIGNAL STATION will be at BATTALION H.Q. AT STRONG POINT "I" and the SIGNAL OFFICER will proceed there immediately on the taking of the BLUE LINE and will take with him two Battalion runners and one runner of the M.G.SECTION who will return to BATTALION H.Q. at STIRLING CASTLE to act as guides.

The method of communication and dealing with prisoners, the use of flares for contact aeroplanes, and orders as to salvage have already been communicated to all concerned.

BATTALION H.Q. will be at STIRLING CASTLE until ZERO + 3 hrs. when it will move to the FORWARD HEADQUARTERS at STRONG POINT "I".

THE MEDICAL AID POST will be at J.13.d.4.0 in a dug out in STIRLING CASTLE.

BRIGADE H.Q. will be in new dug outs in STIRLING CASTLE at about J.13.c.80.10.

H.Q. of 11TH. WEST YORKSHIRE REGT. will be at CLAPHAM JUNCTION at J.13.d.70.70.

H.Q. of 8TH. YORKSHIRE REGT. will be under the MENIN ROAD near NORTHAMPTON FARM until the BLUE LINE has been captured when it will move forward to the German Aid Post at J.20.b.75.90.

H.Q. of 13TH. DURHAM LIGHT INFANTRY will be at TOR TOP SUBWAY until ZERO + 3 hours when it will move forward to the German Dug Out at J.20.b.55.35.

The position of the H.Q. 6TH. BATTALION AUSTRALIAN INFANTRY will be notified later.

9. DRESS - Fighting Order as laid down in Brigade Order No. Less entrenching tool helve and carrier which have been dumped at Q.M.Stores.

10. One day's dry rations plus the emergency ration will be carried by all ranks.

The greatest care will be taken to see that all waterbottles are filled at the start from at RAILWAY DUG OUTS. "C" and "D" Coys. will each carry an extra 50 waterbottles filled.

O's.C.Coys. will be held responsible that all empty petrol tins are returned to the RATION DUMP at the earliest possible moment. Every man going back from the Line to the Ration Dump will carry at least four empty petrol tins or some salvage.

The Battalion RATION DUMP will be formed at some place on the reverse slope of the HILL in INVERNESS COPSE. Position will be notified later.

The Reserve Coy. of the 8TH. YORKSHIRE REGIMENT near BATTALION H.Q. will detail one officer and 60 O.R. on and after "F and "G" Night to carry rations from the BATTALION DUMP to Battalion H.Q. at STRONG POINT "I". Each Coy. in the line will arrange for one N.C.O. and 12 men to fetch its rations from Battalion H.Q. Each party will carry in two trips.

11. The REGIMENTAL POLICE will provide three STRAGGLERS POSTS of two men each who will be posted at intervals in front of the BLUE LINE to see that no men of this Battalion or "D" Coy. 8TH. YORKSHIRE REGIMENT turn back without authority.

12. One runner and one man per coy. will be detailed to report to Battalion H.Q. at STIRLING CASTLE when their coys. are in position at YEOMANRY POST AND SANCTUARY WOOD and will remain there.

13. All BATTLE STORES will be drawn and issued on "D" DAY before the move from MICMAC CAMP. The Qr.Master will arrange with O's.C. Coys. the hour at which they will be drawn.

Tea will be served prior to the start from MICMAC CAMP and hot dinners prior to the start from RAILWAY DUG OUTS.

~~All ranks will take as much rest as possible during "D" Day and prior to the attack.~~

~~Great care will be taken to take all ammunition, rations,~~

-4-

14. All ranks will take as much rest as possible during "D" day and prior to the attack.

15. Great care will be taken to take all ammunition, rations, compasses, field glasses, etc. off all casualties.

16. BLUE FLAGS will be issued to Coys. to be placed at Dug-outs which have been cleared and not occupied.

RED FLAGS will be placed against Dug-outs in which chemical or "P" Bombs have been used and cannot therefore be occupied for a time.

17. O's.C. Coys. will take particular care that casualty, intelligence and situation reports are in punctually to the times required.

(Signed) L.R. PHILLIPS.
Capt. and Adjutant.

18.9.1917.

Copies to
1. File.
2. O.C. "A" Coy.
3. O.C. "B" "
4. O.C. "C" "
5. O.C. "D" "
6. Medical Officer.
7. Quartermaster.
8. Transport Officer.
9. Signalling Officer.
10. Intelligence Officer.
11. H.Q. 69th. Infantry Brigade.
12. 13th. Bn. Durham Light Infantry.
13. 8th. Bn. Australian Infantry.
14. 11th. Bn. West Yorkshire Regiment.
15. 9th. Bn. Yorkshire Regiment.
16. 6th. Bn. Yorkshire Regiment.
17. 69th. Machine Gun Company.
18. 194th. Machine Gun Company.
19. 69th. Trench Mortar Battery.
20. War Diary.

XI W York Regt

Army Form C. 2118.

WAR DIARY
or
INTELLIGENCE SUMMARY.
(Erase heading not required.)

Place	Date	Hour	Summary of Events and Information	Remarks and references to Appendices
INVERNESS COPSE SECTOR	Oct 1st		Battalion in INVERNESS COPSE Sector. Heavy concentration shelling for by enemy. Enemy launched attacks along front but settled from SE & into Army practice barrage and annihilating shoot. In addition to harassing fire and barrage. Battery work. Battalion relieved by 11th Worcesters. Relief commenced 6 pm and completed at 9.45 pm. No casualties during relief. Battalion moved to CANAL BANK in relief in approx there.	
RIDGE WOOD	2nd		Battalion moved from CANAL BANK to RIDGE WOOD	
BERTHEN AREA	3rd		Battalion moved by motor buses to Berthen Area via at Meteren. X.Y.Z.	
	4th 6 pm		Battalion in training. Cleaning up, inspection and re-organisation. Accommodation on 6th Church Parade on 7th	
RENINGHELST	9th		Battalion moved at one hour's notice by motor to ALBERTA CAMP Reninghelst. Remainder commanding of 70th Brigade.	
DICKEBUSCH	10th		Moved from ALBERTA CAMP to Camp "O" Dickebusch.	
CLAPHAM JUNCTION	11th		Moved into Support Positions. HQ A B & C coys at CLAPHAM JUNCTION. D coy at ZILLEBEKE BUND	
FRONT LINE	12th		Battalion relieved 9th York & Lancs Regt in left Battalion front sector	

Army Form C. 2118.

WAR DIARY
or
INTELLIGENCE SUMMARY.
(Erase heading not required.)

Instructions regarding War Diaries and Intelligence Summaries are contained in F.S. Regs., Part II. and the Staff Manual respectively. Title pages will be prepared in manuscript.

Place	Date	Hour	Summary of Events and Information	Remarks and references to Appendices
FRONT LINE	12/15 14th/15		Relief of 9th Inf. Batt. not completed till night of 13/14th and march quickly. Enemy shelled approach lines at 5-6 p.m. A Coy had twenty casualties. Coys. Capt. Smith & Lieut Graham killed. Reinforcements up to Cdr. & Roth's were proceeded to on night of 15/16. Battalion relieved in front line by 8 Argyle & Sutherland Highlanders from CLAPHAM JUNCTION.	
ZILLEBEKE BUND II	16th		Battalion moved from CLAPHAM JUNCTION to ZILLEBEKE BUND.	
ENGLISH WOOD	17/19		Battalion moved to Camp at ENGLISH WOOD on 17th-18th - 19th Spent in cleaning up armament & equipment. Company Drill.	
ZILLEBEKE BUND	19th		Much attention to known wire in areas of Menin Road (Sept 20/21st) practiced by Batt. Bn. Major Sm. J.R. Rushing his Battalion moved from ENGLISH CAMP to ZILLEBEKE BUND, occupying the old positions to the line in support to B. Pot. in Right sector Company.	
FRONT LINE	20		Battalion moved forward to front line.	
	Sept 21 22		Battalion in front line position. No casualties during relief. Relay carried by 3/4 Enemy shelled heavily at times casualties light by 3/4th Queen's of Div. Relieved in former position on night of 22/23rd & moved to reserve	
ZILLEBEKE BUND			Position at ZILLEBEKE BUND.	
WIZERNES	23rd		Battalion entrained at YPRES STATION and proceeded to WIZERNES, where they remained for the night.	
MORINGHEM	24		Moved from WIZERNES to MORINGHEM by motor.	

Army Form C. 2118.

WAR DIARY
or
INTELLIGENCE SUMMARY.
(Erase heading not required.)

Instructions regarding War Diaries and Intelligence Summaries are contained in F. S. Regs., Part II. and the Staff Manual respectively. Title pages will be prepared in manuscript.

Place	Date	Hour	Summary of Events and Information	Remarks and references to Appendices
MORING HEN	26"		General cleaning up. Inspection of Workshops. Stores reorganisation.	
	27"		General cleaning up of Company Lines &c	
	27		Battalion march. "A" Company O 1st b. Preparations being made for Inspection by Field Marshal Sir Douglas Haig, Commander in Chief.	
	28		Tehran Parade. Cleaning up.	
	29		Inspection by H.R.H. Prince of Wales. Draft of 37 O.R. joined from 20th own Camp of 10th Corps Draft Battalion 16 Arras.	
	30		Draft Company O Rangoon O 1st b. Company training & Rifle Drill	
	31		Inspection by the Commander-in-Chief. Announced on parade that the Division had been selected to go to Italy.	

K.T. Sanderson Lieut-Col
O.C. 11 Bn West Yorkshire Regt

www.ingramcontent.com/pod-product-compliance
Lightning Source LLC
Chambersburg PA
CBHW081529160426
43191CB00011B/1718